Routledge Revivals

Sir Philip Sidney and the Interpretation of Renaissance Culture

First published in 1984, *Sir Philip Sidney and the Interpretation of Renaissance Culture* is a collection of essays which reflect the diversity of contemporary approaches to the controversial figure of Sir Philip Sidney, and range from the 'historicist' to the 'revisionist'. Interest in the work of Sir Philip Sidney, in the cultural significance of his 'Circle' in the late Elizabethan age and the following years, has always been a subject of interest. Ever since Sidney's friend Fulke Greville saw his early death as a watershed in English history, the place of this aristocratic poet in literary, cultural and even popular tradition has been momentous. Elevated to mythological status by his contemporaries who survived, he has not lost his power to attract and charm readers of all kids. This book will be of interest to students of literature and history.

Sir Philip Sidney and the Interpretation of Renaissance Culture

The Poet in his Time and in Ours
A Collection of Critical and Scholarly Essays

Edited by Gray F. Waller & Michael D. Moore

First published in 1984
By Croom Helm Ltd

This edition first published in 2024 by Routledge
4 Park Square, Milton Park, Abingdon, Oxon, OX14 4RN
and by Routledge
605 Third Avenue, New York, NY 10017

Routledge is an imprint of the Taylor & Francis Group, an informa business

© 1984 G. F. Waller and M. D. Moore

All rights reserved. No part of this book may be reprinted or reproduced or utilised in any form or by any electronic, mechanical, or other means, now known or hereafter invented, including photocopying and recording, or in any information storage or retrieval system, without permission in writing from the publishers.

Publisher's Note
The publisher has gone to great lengths to ensure the quality of this reprint but points out that some imperfections in the original copies may be apparent.

Disclaimer
The publisher has made every effort to trace copyright holders and welcomes correspondence from those they have been unable to contact.

A Library of Congress record exists under ISBN: 0389205141

ISBN: 978-1-032-72962-6 (hbk)
ISBN: 978-1-003-42324-9 (ebk)
ISBN: 978-1-032-72963-3 (pbk)

Book DOI 10.4324/9781003423249

Sir Philip Sidney and the Interpretation of Renaissance Culture

THE POET IN HIS TIME AND IN OURS

A Collection of Critical and Scholarly Essays

Edited by
GARY F. WALLER
&
MICHAEL D. MOORE

CROOM HELM
London & Sydney

BARNES & NOBLE BOOKS
Totowa, New Jersey

© 1984 G.F. Waller and M.D. Moore
Croom Helm Ltd, Provident House, Burrell Row,
Beckenham Kent BR3 1AT

Croom Helm Australia Pty Ltd, First Floor,
139 King Street, Sydney, NSW 2001, Australia

British Library Cataloguing in Publication Data

Sir Philip Sidney and the interpretation
  of Renaissance culture.
  1. Sidney, *Sir* Philip–Criticism and
  interpretation
  I. Waller, Gary F. II. Moore, Michael D.
  821'.3   PR2343
  ISBN 0-7099-2788-6

First published in the USA 1984 by
Barnes & Noble Books,
81 Adams Drive,
Totowa, New Jersey, 07512

Library of Congress Cataloguing in Publication Data
Main entry under title:

Sir Philip Sidney and the interpretation of Renaissance culture.
  1. Sidney, Philip, Sir, 1554-1586 – Criticism and
interpretation – Addresses, essays, lectures. 2. Rennaissance
– Addresses, essays, lectures. I. Waller, Gary.
II. Moore, Michael
PR2343.S57   1984   821'.3   84-12343
ISBN 0-389-20514-1

Printed and bound in Great Britain

CONTENTS

Introduction
Credits
Contributors

PART I   THE POET IN HIS TIME . . .   1

    Speaking Pictures: Sidney's Rapprochement
    between Poetry and Painting, *by S.K. Heninger, Jr*   3

    The Meeting of the Muses: Sidney and the
    Mid-Tudor Poets, *by Germaine Warkentin*   17

    Divided Aims in the *Revised Arcadia*,
    by Maurice Evans   34

    Astrophil's Stella and Stella's Astrophil,
    by Robert L. Montgomery   44

    Sidneian Indirection: The Ethical Irony of
    Astrophil and Stella, *by Charles S. Levy*   56

PART II   . . . AND IN OURS   67

    The Rewriting of Petrarch: Sidney and the
    Languages of Sixteenth-Century Poetry,
    by Gary F. Waller   69

    Unending Desire: Sidney's Reinvention of
    Petrarchan Form in *Astrophil and Stella*,
    by Marion Campbell   84

    'What May Words Say': The Limits of Language
    in *Astrophil and Stella*, *by Jacqueline T. Miller* 95

Contents

    Sidney's Presence in Lyric Verse of the
    Later English Renaissance, *by Jon A. Quitslund*   110

    The Cultural Politics of the *Defence of Poetry*,   124
    by Alan Sinfield

INDEX   145

INTRODUCTION

       Most of these essays originated as papers presented to
the International Conference, 'Sir Philip Sidney in His
History and Ours,' held at Wilfrid Laurier University,
Waterloo, Canada, in October 1982. Additional essays have
been commissioned to fill out the collection so that it expresses what we believe is a representative selection of the
most interesting work currently being done on Sidney and the
Sidney Circle. The editors are especially grateful to the
authors of the specially commissioned essays which were re-
quested when some of the conference papers proved impossible
or were unavailable to publish. All are indications that at
approximately the 400th anniversary of Sidney's death, interest in and important study of Sidney and the Sidney Circle
seems to be increasing. The emphasis of both the Laurier
conference and this volume of essays likewise suggests the
new importance of Sidney in our rewriting of Renaissance
literary and cultural history. Critics and scholars from
Britain, Canada, the United States and Australia are represented here and, like the conference itself, the collection
of papers expresses a diversity of scholarly and critical
approaches. This variety is reflected in the joint focus of
the volume's title, as it was in the title of the conference.
The dividing line we have attempted to draw between 'Sidney's'
History and 'Ours' is, of course, arbitrary: all considerations of his life and work are by definition in 'our'
history. But in general in the first group we have those
essays which employ the traditional methods of contextual
historicism and in the second those that attempt, in different ways, to break beyond the limits of traditional empiricist historicism and whose methodology arises from the
demands and questions of 'our' history. Of course, Sidney,
his contemporaries, and readers today are all contributors to
the same history.
       The editors of this volume, who also organized the con-
ference, wish to thank a number of institutions and indivi-

Introduction

duals. We gratefully acknowledge the help, in diverse capacities, of A.C. Hamilton, Stuart Hunter, Linda Levine, Gerald D. Rubio, Roger Kuin, William A. Sessions, and for research and preparation of the manuscript, Amy Goodwin in Pittsburgh, and Susan Rudy and Charlotte Cox in Waterloo. We also wish to thank the Departments of English at Carnegie-Mellon University and Wilfrid Laurier University for providing research assistance and secretarial services. Finally, both editors would like to express thanks to the Social Sciences and Humanities Research Council of Canada and to Wilfrid Laurier University for the generous financial help which made possible both the conference and the publication of these essays.

> Gary F. Waller, Department of English
> Carnegie-Mellon University
>
> Michael D. Moore, Department of English
> Wilfrid Laurier University

CREDITS

Permission to quote from the following standard editions is gratefully acknowledged. Throughout, these works are abbreviated as *Poems*, *Old Arcadia*, and *Misc. Prose* respectively, and page or other references are incorporated into the text.

The Poems of Sir Philip Sidney, edited by William A. Ringler, Jr (Oxford: The Clarendon Press, 1962).

The Countess of Pembroke's Arcadia (the Old Arcadia), edited with an introduction and commentary by Jean Robertson (Oxford: The Clarendon Press, 1973).

Miscellaneous Prose of Sir Philip Sidney, edited by Katherine Duncan-Jones and Jan van Dorsten (Oxford: The Clarendon Press, 1973).

CONTRIBUTORS

Marion Campbell is Tutor in English, University of Melbourne, Australia. She has published in such journals as *Southern Review* and *English Literary History*, and is completing a study of unfinished works in the Renaissance.

Maurice Evans is Professor Emeritus, University of Exeter. His many publications include the Penguin *Arcadia*, *Sixteenth Century Poetry* (Hutchinson University Library) and *Spenser's Anatomy of Heroism* (Cambridge).

S.K. Heninger, Jr is Professor of English, University of North Carolina. He has written many books and articles, including *'Touches of Sweet Harmony'* (Huntingdon), *A Handbook of Renaissance Meteorology* (North Carolina) and many other studies in the Renaissance, including a forthcoming work on the poetics of Spenser and Sidney.

Charles S. Levy is Associate Professor of English, Cornell University. He is the editor of the forthcoming Clarendon Press edition of Sidney's letters, and of articles on Sidney.

Jacqueline T. Miller is Assistant Professor of English, Rutgers University. She has written articles on Sidney, Spenser, Renaissance poetical theory in such journals as *English Literary History* and *Sidney Newsletter*.

Robert L. Montgomery is Professor of English, University of California at Irvine. He is the author of *Symmetry and Sense*, a study of Sidney's poetry, and of other studies in the Renaissance, includiing *The Reader's Eye: Studies in Didactic Literary Theory from Dante to Tasso*.

Michael D. Moore is Assistant Professor of English, Wilfrid Laurier University, Waterloo, Canada. In addition to his interests in the Renaissance, he has published on nineteenth-century literature, notably Newman and Hopkins.

Contributors

Jon A. Quitslund is Assistant Professor of English, George Washington University, Washington, D.C. He has written many articles on Renaissance literature, especially on neo-Platonism.

Alan Sinfield is Senior Lecturer in English, University of Sussex. He has written books and articles on Renaissance literature, nineteenth- and twentieth-century literature and culture, and literary theory. His most recent books are *Dramatic Monologue* (Methuen), *Poetry and Politics 1580-1640* and *Society and Literature 1945-1970* (Croom Helm), and he has a book on Tennyson forthcoming with Blackwell.

Gary F. Waller is Professor of Literary Studies and Head of the Department of English, Carnegie-Mellon University. He is the author of several books on Renaissance literature including *Mary Sidney Countess of Pembroke* (Salzburg) and a study of sixteenth-century poetry in the Longmans Literature in English series. He has also published widely in contemporary literature and literary theory.

Germaine Warkentin is Associate Professor of English, Victoria College, University of Toronto. She has published widely on Renaissance and Canadian literature, and is currently preparing a translation of Petrarch and completing a work on Petrarchan sonnet sequences.

THE POET IN HIS TIME . . .

SPEAKING PICTURES: SIDNEY'S RAPPROCHEMENT BETWEEN POETRY AND PAINTING

S.K. Heninger, Jr

Like Alan Sinfield in his contribution to this collection of essays, I'm concerned to deal with the inconsistencies and contradictions in *The defence of poesie*. But whereas Sinfield argues in terms of Sidney responding to a complex politics which emerged from a developing Protestantism, I'm prone to talk in philosophical terms, and I look for the way in which Sidney responded to the changing answer to the question of 'What is real?' According to the old answer, ultimate reality lay among the essences in a Platonic world of being or among the attributes of God in a Christian heaven. But increasingly the answer was being given by empiricists that reality lay among the palpable phenomena of physical nature. So Sidney's treatise, as I read it, is an attempt to adjust to this shifting ontology.

The sixteenth century witnessed vast changes in the culture of Western Europe. Revolutions in cosmology, in theology, and in psychology reinforced one another to produce what is broadly called the scientific revolution of the following century. There were, of course, commensurately large changes in artistic theory, occasioned by the same sweeping forces that shaped what we from our vantage point see as the modern era. Just as empiricism led to experimental science and man-centered religions and democratic societies, so in the arts it led to genre painting and the novel. An artifact was no longer the embodiment of an anterior truth brought down from heaven, as it had been for centuries under the Christianized version of Platonic esthetics: rather, the artifact now recorded a congeries of observed data on earth.

To understand *The defence of poesie* we must see it in this contemporary context. Proponents of the new esthetics had resurrected Aristotle's *Poetics*, which they were touting as license for a mimetic theory of art that trained the poet's eye on observable nature. Sidney responded to the crisis in literary studies brought about by the recovery of Aristotle's *Poetics* and immediately recognized its implications for making the poet a self-conscious artificer rather than a mystically inspired seer. And while he wished to maintain an allegiance to that portion of the Platonic tradition which extolled poetry and acknowledged it as an acculturating agent for the improvement of society, he nonetheless chose to implement the Aristotelian doctrine of art as mimesis because it offered a means of making literature more effective in its political purpose.[1]

As a result, *The defence of poesie* is a manifesto which is at once conservative and radical--conservative in its motives, but radical in the means by which it seeks to achieve those purposes. It draws heavily upon the Platonic tradition to perpetuate the age-old view that poetry should be directed toward the furthering of both public and private virtue, but it also contentiously advocates a new mechanism for poetry based upon Aristotelian mimesis and proposes a radical revision of the previous relationship between poet and poem and reader. Although in the *defence* Sidney repeatedly pays deference to Plato--'of all philosophers,' he says, 'I have ever esteemed [him] most worthy of reverence' (*Misc. Prose*, p. 107)--Sidney gives his most forthright and concise definition of poetry in Aristotelian terms. Quite early in the *defence*, in one of his most forceful pronouncements, Sidney declares: 'Poesy . . . is an art of imitation, for so Aristotle termeth it in the word μίμησις' (79.35-6): and by way of a gloss, he continues by adding that poetry is also a 'speaking picture' (80.2). This statement encapsulates the fundamental principle of Sidney's poetics, providing a baseline for the discussion that follows.

Nonetheless, Sidney is always aware of the earlier esthetic and continually makes concessions to it. His intention, in fact, is to moderate between the old and the new, to offer a continuity that will allow innovation in the direction of empiricism without renouncing the achievements of the past that ennoble poetry and make it a praiseworthy discipline. In this way, *The defence of poesie* encompasses the crisis in literary theory which took place in the sixteenth century. Properly located, it should be seen as a contribution to the changes which occurred as the neoplatonic esthetic which prevailed at the beginning of the century was challenged and eventually replaced by an empiricist esthetic which evolved from a biased interpretation of Aristotle's *Poetics*.

What I shall do in this essay, then, is to sketch the shift in esthetic postulates between 1500 and 1600 as they bore upon literary theory, emphasizing the important role that the recovery of Aristotle's *Poetics* played in this transition. Then, I shall suggest the relevance that the concept of speaking pictures had in the accompanying debate. My ulterior intention, though, is to demonstrate how Sidney exploited the rapprochement between poetry and painting in order to achieve his political purpose of moving men to virtuous action.

So what major changes did occur in literary theory during Sidney's lifetime? Broadly speaking, at the beginning of the sixteenth century artistic theory was still dominated by the neoplatonic esthetic inherited from the Middle Ages and reinvigorated by the quattrocento Florentines under the tutelage of Marsilio Ficino and Cristoforo Landino.[2] In the act of composition, the poet, guided by the Muses, underwent a *furor poeticus* during which he was privileged to witness directly the eternal verities in some transcendental realm of ideas. His task was then to embody these verities, commonly subsumed under the comprehensive term 'heavenly beauty,' in a form which would make these elusive values knowable to his fellowmen. In this task, fortunately, the poet enjoyed an example in the deity who had created our universe. According to Timaeus, Plato's best-known authority on cosmology, when the deity created our universe he used as his model this idea of heavenly beauty, which he proceeded to express mathematically through the disposition of the cosmos. In biblical terms, frequently repeated in the Renaissance, he created according to number, weight, and measure; and the heavenly beauty which the creating deity used as his model is manifest in the proportion and harmony evident everywhere in the world that lies about us. As a moral imperative, therefore, in emulation of the heavenly maker, the poet in the creation of his fictive universe should follow this divine example. And as an esthetic imperative, in order to make his artifact artistically acceptable, the poet must endow his poem with proportion and harmony, the mathematical display of cosmic perfection. In order to represent heavenly beauty accurately, the poet must like the deity compose according to number, weight, and measure--that is, he must metrify his work. So metrics in poetry is not an incidental nicety applied *post facto*; rather, it is a *sine qua non*, the quiddity of poetry, because proportion and harmony are the essential criteria of artistic excellence.

In this poetics, the mode of existence of the poem resides at some transcendent level with its idea, heavenly beauty. But this insubstantial concept is rendered manifest by the mathematics of proportion and harmony, which produce a form inhabiting an ambiguous intermundum between concept and percept. The reader, of course, has available only the percept of the poem--its phenomena, its content. But in such a poem, content is merely ancillary to form--or perhaps, content is a metaphor for form, the means by which form is made knowable. The experience of reading, then, involves apprehension of the subject matter only as a means of comprehending the proportion and harmony that reveal the form. And in turn, comprehension of the inner form leads to an awareness of the concept of heavenly beauty, which is the poem's originating idea, eternally resident in a Platonic world of essences or in a Christian heaven. Dante's *Divina commedia* with its *terza rima* and its three books leading to God's presence is a poem of this sort.

Such an esthetic is invariably optimistic. The artifact always looks to cosmic perfection as its model and always reflects, no matter how remotely, the concept of heavenly beauty. For this reason, Platonic poets necessarily describe a golden world.

And the reader is invited to escape into this golden world for an acquaintance with the ideal. The process of reading leads to an experience which is parallel to but the reverse of the *furor poeticus* of the poet when he is inspired by the Muses. The process of comprehending a poem induces a corresponding frenzy in the reader—a *divino furore*, to use Landino's phrase—which raises him in ecstasy to an immediate experience of the heavenly beauty which the poem embodies. A poem, like any true artifact in this esthetic, through its proportion and harmony activates the innate harmony in the soul of the reader so that he resonates in unison with the world-soul. The poem allows the reader to reunify with the transcendent world of eternal verities, reminds him of his place of origin, his celestial home. Spenser assumes this poetics in the October eclogue when he proposes a poetic theory of *enthusiasmos*, and Sidney reveals a ready sympathy with it when he talks about the mind of a reader being 'lift [ed] up . . . from the dungeon of the body to the enjoying his own divine essence' (82.26-7).

The weight of this tradition was enormous and could not be easily pushed aside. In time, though, it proved noisome to humanists, especially those later ones with a scientific curiosity, because they wanted to consider things in the context of this world rather than the next. It was noisome also to many artificers, especially painters and sculptors, whose art depended increasingly on what the eye observes as it looks about. Following this trend which placed reality among the objects of physical nature and removed it from the realm of celestial ideas, the poets also sought a theory which would justify the description of things as they appear to the senses and would release the poet from the monotonous repetition of heavenly harmonies. In Aristotle's *Poetics* they found a handy authority to serve their turn. They seized upon Aristotle's cardinal tenet, announced in the opening paragraph of the *Poetics*, that poetry is an art of imitation; and they boldly clarified the somewhat cloudy point in Aristotle that the appropriate object of poetic imitation is not some insubstantial idea beyond our grasp, but rather the wholly visible actions of men.

Sidney himself had severe reservations about the neo-platonic view of poetry as divine frenzy. For a Protestant, the desire to apprehend celestial forms was unacceptably close to intrusion upon the fearsome Deity. The *furor poeticus* seemed presumptuous on the part of the poet, a claim to creativity that encroached upon the uniqueness of the godhead and saucily competed with Nature, God's vice-regent on earth (79. 12-7). It also tempted the reader, lifting him beyond the acceptable limits of human knowledge. The *divino furore* was dangerous, releasing the reader from the rule of reason and catapulting him into a world of unbridled emotion. In consequence, in his more guarded moments Sidney renounced the extreme belief in poetic ecstasy and distanced himself from Plato--'especially since,' Sidney says, 'he attributeth unto poesy more than myself do, namely, to be a very inspiring of a divine force, far above man's wit' (109.2-4).

Clearly, Sidney's attitude toward Plato was equivocal. He wished to retain those tenets of neoplatonism which proclaim poetry to be a noble art, uplifting and refining, the producer of golden worlds that our erected wit can appreciate. But lest the poet becomes too saucy and panders to our infected will, the soaring esthetics of the Florentines had to be curtailed. Poetry must remain within the human sphere. 'They that delight in poesy itself,' Sidney warns, 'should seek to know what they do, and how they do; and especially look themselves in an unflattering glass of reason' (111.25-7). Poetry must be a wholly human product, and must induce a wholly human experience within the bounds of man's limited wit.

So Sidney explicitly rejected the neoplatonic esthetic of divine inspiration and joined with the advocates of Aristotle. As we have seen, poetry for Sidney before all else was an art of imitation as Aristotle had defined it in the term *mimesis*. Unabashedly, Sidney aligned himself with the growing number of neo-Aristotelians and entered the heated debate over just what Aristotle might have meant by his statement that poetry first and foremost must be mimetic--a statement, incidentally, that engaged the Renaissance to a much greater extent than any theory of tragedy, and rightly so, because it is fundamental to an empiricist poetic.

When we examine the Aristotelian text--and after Robortello's edition in 1548 it was examined with extreme care--we find that Aristotle is rather vague about mimesis, and therefore he submits to a high degree of speculative interpretation. Imitation is the distinguishing feature of poetry, and the object of this imitation without question should be the actions of men. From this derives the notion of plot, a sequence of episodes presenting the actions of a man as an integrated whole; and since some one must perform those actions, the notion of character follows in the wake of the necessity for plot. But exactly what Aristotle means by the actions of men and exactly how the verbal medium of poetry is to accomplish this imitation are far from clear. Aristotle seems to imply no more than that plot, the most important element in a poem, should be the representation of an action which reveals what might be or should be according to probability or necessity. Although he does not rule out an actual occurrence as an acceptable object for poetic imitation, the actual occurrence must nonetheless be rendered universal—that is, the historical event must be typical, representing what might be or should be according to probability or necessity.

Interpretation of the concept *mimesis* became the center of the storm that raged around the *Poetics* with increasing fury as the sixteenth century wore on, and what Aristotle might have meant by it was subjected to every refinement of subtle argument as well as to the bluster of not so subtle assertion. The crux of the problem lay in the interdependency between poetic fiction and the new reality of physical phenomena. If a poet did not record an actual occurrence, his poem had no basis in fact. His poem was made-up, divorced from truth, so that the word 'artificial,' previously adulatory, came to imply deceptiveness, and the word 'fiction' acquired its modern implication of 'fictitious.'

The easiest solution to this dilemma was simply to assume that the poet would limit himself to what he had actually observed, in accord with the rising empiricism of the period, and this assumption led inevitably to realism. Aristotle's dictum that poetry should be an imitation of the actions of men readily transmuted to a principle that poetry should describe men in action. This interpretation led quickly to the conclusion that a poem should be an imitation of a particular action that has taken place--until finally, by the time of Dryden, we can see in the preface to his *Annus Mirabilis* that the 'historical poem,' to use Dryden's phrase, has become a major genre and has stolen preeminence even from the epic.[3]

Sidney, of course, was writing almost a century before Dryden, and he is far less advanced in the progress toward realism. But the movement toward depictive poetry was well under way and the outcome is already discernible in *The defence of poesie*. In a key passage of his argument, Sidney renounces metrification as a requirement for poetry, just as elsewhere he renounces other features of the neoplatonic esthetic. Although 'the greatest part of poets have apparelled their poetical inventions in that numbrous kind of writing which is called verse' (81.22-4), as Sidney reminds us, this remark is occasioned by his radical assertion that 'verse. . .[is] but an ornament and no cause to poetry.' In Sidney's syncretic poetics, he is willing to recognize the beauty that metrification lends to a poem, but such formal properties are extraneous and not intrinsic to poetry. They are 'an ornament and no cause to poetry.' Instead, 'it is that feigning notable images of virtues, vices, or what else . . . which must be the right describing note to know a poet by' (81.36-82.1).

Sidney, then, was in the vanguard of those who transformed poetry into a primarily descriptive and narrative art, largely an image-producing activity. He had found in the recently recovered *Poetics* of Aristotle a ready instrument for achieving this revolution in poetic theory. Whereas under the old dispensation poetry was at basis a formal art identified by its metrics, under the new dispensation poetry became a pictorial art, locating events in the phenomenal world. Whereas at the beginning of the sixteenth century, music was the art most closely allied to poetry because of their shared formal properties—by the end of the sixteenth century the sister art of poetry was painting.

This realignment among siblings in the family of the arts was a predictable consequence of the triumph of Aristotelian poetics, and Sidney's juxtaposition of the term *mimesis* and the phrase 'speaking picture' is neither casual nor by chance. After the mid-sixteenth century, the assertion that poetry is a speaking picture, a *pictura loquens*, appeared with increasing frequency in discussions of artistic theory, and indeed was soon tossed about with the unexamined certainty of a self-evident truth. That poetry is a speaking picture, a visual image with semantic import, and the corollary, always understood if not always stated, that painting is a silent poesy, epitomized the emerging empiricist esthetic. Bolstered by the phrase *ut pictura poesis*, timely ripped from Horace, it proclaimed the radical doctrine that poetry most of all is like the verisimilar art of painting. Both poetry and painting are arts of imitation, producing images. Poetry, in fact, is no more than a 'speaking picture,' a painting with semantic content that has been verbalized.

Although such an assertion may appear glib to us, lax and inaccurate and indefinable, the phrase 'speaking picture' had enjoyed a long and precise tradition which Sidney was fully aware of. He took it seriously; and especially given the Aristotelian context in which it appears in *The defence of poesie*, it might well provide the readiest approach to the novel proposals which Sidney makes for poetry. Certainly, it behooves us to ask what freight of meaning the phrase carried in the sixteenth century.

Plutarch is the originating authority for this topos in its best known formulation. He mentions it in several places, but deals with it most extensively in the essay, 'Whether the Athenians were more renowned for martiall armes or good letters,' as Philemon Holland translated it in 1603. As his authority, in turn, Plutarch reverentially cites a predecessor, Simonides of Ceos, the great lyric poet, who reportedly had said (again, in the words of Holland): 'Picture was a dumbe poesie, and poesie a speaking picture.'[4] In this essay, Plutarch is at pains to show that although the Athenians are famous for their achievements in philosophy, art, and literature, they are even more remarkable for their military feats;

and it provides a fixed point of reference for assessing the complementarity of poetry and history, a relationship which had been of considerable concern to Aristotle, and thence to Sidney.

Plutarch's essay begins by noting that men of letters are dependent upon great men of action for their subject matter, a circumstance that Spenser is very much aware of in the October eclogue. According to the direct logic of Plutarch, 'If you take away men of action, you shall be sure to have no writers of them' (Holland, p. 981). Plutarch has in mind the historians, such as Thucydides and Xenophon, whom he mentions. It is their function to record as accurately as possible the brave deeds of soldiers; and thereby the historians achieve a certain nobility themselves: 'For surely there is a certaine image of glorie, which by a kinde of reflexion, as in a mirrour, doth rebound from those who have atchieved noble acts, even unto them that commit the same to writing.' The similitude between writing history and reflecting events as in a mirror is significant; the emphasis is upon accuracy and completeness in the written report. Obviously, Plutarch is thinking of literature of a certain kind, as an exact image of actuality.

From here, Plutarch glides smoothly into a consideration of painting, another art which records faithfully the activity of battle. As an example, he describes in kinetic detail the famous painting by Euphranor which depicted the Athenian victory over Epaminondas at Mantineia (incidentally, the locale for Sidney's *Arcadia*). But Plutarch's meticulous account of Euphranor's painting is merely preparation for the conclusion that the painting, regardless of its vividness and vitality, is unmistakably derivative, subordinate to the reality it portrays. And it is in this context that painting and poetry are compared. The next sentence cites Simonides to the effect that painting is dumb poesy and poesy is a speaking picture. Although Plutarch uses the word 'poesy' (ποίησις), he is thinking of it as a record of events, in the sense of our word 'history'; and the successful poet will be he who like the painter captures the vivacity of commotion. There is no question that Plutarch is thinking here of poetry as a narrative of events, as ἱστορία. Equally without doubt, his intention is to denigrate poetry. Like painting, poetry is derivative. And just as we are not to prefer 'the wit or judgement of a painter' over 'the courage and polity of a captaine,' so we are not to prize a victory ode over the glorious trophies of war. A painting or a poem is but a 'vaine shadow,' says Plutarch, that palls in the presence of 'the reall substance and thing indeed.'

But Plutarch's original context for Simonides' statement was willingly forgotten, and the way that *historia* evolved to *storia* and thence to 'story,' a fictive narrative, allowed Sidney to write the *Arcadia* within the tradition of poetry as a speaking picture. As this tradition developed, a poem is simply an account of human affairs with a wealth of depictive details. Like a picture, it must give the illusion of a lively reality. The justification for poetry, in fact, is this capacity for lifelike fiction. Although poetry is inferior to painting in its ability to represent a busy scene with compelling veracity, 'even poetry,' as Plutarch conceded, 'hath a grace, and is esteemed, for that it describeth and relateth things as if they had beene done, and which carie a resemblance of truth' (Holland, p. 984).

In Sidney's mind, prompted by Aristotle, this license for the poet to create a fiction that hypothesizes what might be, just so it accords with probability, gave poetry the edge over history, which is confined to the facts of what actually has been (87.30-91.2). Nonetheless, according to this theory poetry is like painting in its depictive properties, and it easily complies with Aristotle's injunction that poetry imitate the actions of men. A poem by definition becomes an account of human affairs, a sequence of enjambed episodes, a continuous narrative. So literature, including both history and poetry, should strive for verisimilitude. And although language cannot fully reproduce physical reality, and in this attempt poetry and even history are inferior to painting, nevertheless in literary treatises since the mid-sixteenth century Plutarch's *pictura loquens* had been supplemented with Horace's *ut pictura poesis* to insist that poetry, like painting, can be successful to a high degree in the production of images.

Converging upon this point-of-view from another direction was a widely held theory of painting that saw the picture as a window through which one observes an action which has been suddenly arrested in process by the artist. Since Alberti's *Della pittura* in the 1430s, a notion of painting had developed similarly dependent upon the concept of *historia*. In this theory, a painting is expected to capture the significant moment in a continuous action, implying what came before and after this moment, and thereby conveying the significance of the entire event.[5] Largely through the stance and gestures of the figures in the painting, their thoughts and feelings--their 'attitudes'--are revealed, and thereby what they 'mean' is expressed.

Sidney shows familiarity with this theory of painting when he uses a picture of the suicidal Lucrece as an illustration for his notion of 'right poetry.' He describes 'the constant though lamenting look of Lucretia, when she punished in herself another's fault'; and he notes that the artist 'painteth not Lucretia whom he never saw, but painteth the outward beauty of such a virtue' (80.34-81.2)--that is, he paints the way her inner qualities would manifest themselves as beauty to the eye. By the outer beauty of Lucrece displayed in the painting, the artist describes her inner virtue.

Speaking Pictures

The painting becomes a definition of virtue. To use the pertinent half of Plutarch's formula, painting is a silent poesy. The painting encapsulates the meaning of the narrative which has been frozen for the moment within the frame of the picture.

In retrospect, it seemed as though painting and poetry had always been close since the classical period. Painting and poetry were often compared by both Plato and Aristotle, and authors such as Pliny reported the frequent practice of painters who drew their subject matter from a literary text. After Cicero, it was common to speak of Homer as a painter rather than a poet, because he conveyed the scenes of his epics in such convincing detail.[6] Nowhere were painting and poetry drawn more closely together, however, than in the tradition of word-pictures known as *icons* in Greek or *images* in Latin. The prototype of such an artifact is the εἰκόνες of Philostratus the Elder, who flourished in the third century A.D., and a lengthy line of imitators had followed his example. Holding in mind Aristotle's injunction that art should imitate human actions, Philostratus in the opening sentence of his work reveals the impetus for his verbal portraits: 'Whosoever scorns painting is unjust to truth; and he is also unjust to all the wisdom that has been bestowed upon poets-- for poets and painters make equal contribution to our knowledge of the deeds and the looks of heroes.'[7] Philostratus then proceeds to give sixty-five brief portraits of such legendary figures as Phaëton and Pasiphaë, placed in a stereoscopic setting and caught in their most telling act. Each verbal picture is indeed an icon or image--a faithful representation of a memorable topos. The word-artist has painted a picture with language by piling up descriptive details, adding pictorial line after line just as a painter adds stroke after stroke to his canvas until he fills it and compiles a reproduction of what he wishes to portray.

It is likely that Alberti had in mind this tradition for verbal icons when he proposed his theory of painting as *historia*. Certainly Alberti assumed that most of the subjects for painting would be drawn from a mythological source. He mentions, for example, the feigned madness of Ulysses, the battle of Centaurs and Lapiths, and the sacrifice of Iphigeneia. But this theory of painting as *historia* lent itself to an empiricist interpretation, and Alberti's notion of the picture as window inexorably led to the genre painting of the seventeenth century.

By Sidney's day, then, there was a time-honored tradition for interrelating poetry and painting, and for seeing both as semantic systems that borrowed from one another and that were most expressive when used in conjunction. Poetry is a speaking picture, and painting is a dumb poesy. The emblem-book, a distinctive Renaissance genre that appeared on the scene in the 1530s, is a predictable--almost an inevitable--product of this tradition; and Barthélemy Aneau, one of the early emblem-authors, candidly called his collection *Picta poesis,* 'poesy rendered visible in pictures' (Lyons, 1552).

This inclination to meddle painting and poetry was further encouraged by the pervasive discipline of rhetoric, so that every schoolboy learned how to do it. Rhetoric provided a common denominator for the conflation of poetry and painting as semiotic systems. Since the art of speaking well sought to sway an audience, most figures of rhetoric were aimed at producing certain effects, certain experiences for those in attendance at the oration. Many rhetorical figures were designed specifically to create a quasi-visual image so compelling in lifelike detail that it seems to materialize before the very eyes of the listeners--indeed, the audience is transformed into a group of spectators. The audience literally sees what the speaker is painting in words. Rhetorical figures purporting to achieve this effect included *hypotyposis, demonstratio, descriptio, effictio, imago,* and *similitudo.* In discussions of style, all these depictive figures strove to produce an effect known by the Greek term ἐνάργεια or the Latin *evidentia.* From Aristotle through Quintilian to Thomas Wilson, rhetoricians had emphasized the power of ἐνάργεια in presenting a thing, person, or episode so vividly that it affects the audience as an immediate experience.[8] This strategy of creating a visual impression came so naturally to the rhetorician that rhetoric was regularly compared to painting as an image-producing art, and its figures of speech came to be known as 'colors.'

Because of his popularity in the Renaissance, Quintilian is an appropriate authority to explain the theory and practice of those rhetorical figures which by artful illusion create such images. Ἐνάργεια, Quintilian explains,

> . . . or, as some prefer to call it, representation [*evidentia*], is something more than mere clearness, since the latter merely lets itself be seen, whereas the former thrusts itself upon our notice. It is a great gift to be able to set forth the facts on which we are speaking clearly and vividly. For oratory fails of its full effect, and does not assert itself as it should if its appeal is merely to the hearing, and if the judge merely feels that the facts on which he has to give his decision are being narrated to him, and not displayed in their living truth to the eyes of the mind (VIII.iii.61-2).

The vivid description, in Quintilian's words, is directed to 'the eyes of the mind,' the *oculi mentis*, an inner-oriented faculty for seeing earlier identified by Cicero.[9] To accommodate the word-picture drawn by the orator, to explain how the purely verbal is translated into the convincingly visual, Quintilian predicates the existence of some auxiliary sense

Speaking Pictures

faculty, the mind's eye.

From here the topos of the *oculi mentis* became a commonplace, a basic assumption that conditioned all discourse. In a passage of extreme importance for rendering poetry respectable, Erasmus drew heavily upon Quintilian and adapted the theory to the written rather than the spoken word. Another method of copiousness, Erasmus explains,

> . . . involves ἐνάργεια, which is translated as *evidentia*, 'vividness.' We employ this whenever, for the sake of amplifying or decorating our passage, or giving pleasure to our readers, instead of setting out the subject in bare simplicity, we fill in the colours and set it up like a picture to look at, so that we seem to have painted the scene rather than described it, and the reader seems to have seen rather than read.[10]

After Erasmus, all the arts of discourse, but especially poetry, possessed this potential for producing quasi-visual impressions. It offered its images to 'the mind's eye,' a faculty of the psyche that had been implicit in Aristotle and explicit since Cicero. The reader seems to have seen rather than read.

Sidney concurred in this potential of language to produce images, and he made it a cornerstone of his poetics. In his view, in fact, it is precisely this enargeiac power of the poet which bestows superiority to poetry over philosophy. Whereas philosophy deals only in concepts, operating in some vague realm of generalities, poetry embodies the concept in a concrete example and thereby endows it with palpable properties that render it immediately knowable. 'For whatsoever the philosopher saith should be done,' Sidney argues, the poet 'giveth a perfect picture of it in someone by whom he presupposeth it was done, so as he coupleth the general notion with the particular example' (85.22-6). And Sidney goes on: 'A perfect picture I say, for he yieldeth to the powers of the mind an image of that whereof the philosopher bestoweth but a wordish description, which doth neither strike, pierce, nor possess the sight of the soul so much as that other doth.' In order to embody the generality of the philosopher in the more efficacious form of a concrete example, the poet resorts to the rhetorician's concept of ἐνάργεια, a term that Sidney actually uses elsewhere in the *Defence*.[11] To 'the powers of the mind' the poet offers an image which strikes, pierces, and possesses the *oculi mentis*--'the sight of the soul,' in Sidney's phrase. By this means the poet feigns those notable images of virtues, vices, or what else which must be the right describing note to know a poet by. Not unexpectedly at this point, Sidney draws upon his previous assertion that poetry is a speaking picture, and he concludes this passage by reiterating that the 'learned definitions' of the philosopher 'lie dark before the imaginative and judging power [of the reader's mind], if they be not illuminated or figured forth by the speaking picture of poesy' (86.3-8). To provide such a speaking picture, we may safely assume, Astrophel 'sought fit words to paint the blackest face of woe,' and thereby to sway Stella and perhaps to instruct us, his readers.

In fine, by being a speaking picture, poetry approaches painting in its immediacy as experience which affects the behavior of an audience. Especially when painting is seen as *historia*, the instantaneous revelation of a continuous and consequential action, it allows for this conflation with poetry. There is a rapprochement between these sister arts in their ability to produce a sense-perceptible image with meaning, rather like an emblem. Furthermore, calling upon the suasiveness of rhetoric, this image has an instructive effect upon the reader. By these means poetry conforms to Aristotle's dictum that poetry should imitate the actions of men and it fulfills Sidney's political program that it should lead to virtuous action among the citizenry. The well-knowing of the poet eventuates in the well-doing of the reader, and Sidney's hope for poetry as an agent of moral regeneration is achieved.

So Sidney appears at that node in our cultural history when the prevalent esthetics was turning from a dependence upon the formal criteria of proportion and verging toward an empirical basis in the accurate observation and description of physical nature. Sidney, as an author of songs and sonnets, a humanist, a platonist, looks back nostalgically to a poetics with heavenly beauty as its subject matter and the Muses as its sponsor. As a modern man of practical affairs, a Protestant, an incipient empiricist, he introduces a new poetics where images direct their sensuous appeal to the mind's eye. He inhabits that crucial period when poetry was turning from music as its closest relation in the family of the arts and renewing an alliance with painting. The syncretic poetics which Sidney propounds in the *Defence* is a studied attempt to provide the necessary continuity, retaining the best of the old while allowing the novelty of experiment; and rightly seen, Sidney is the mediator for this invigorating transition not only in England, but in Western Europe at large. The *Arcadia* provided triumphant proof that a poem is not primarily a metrical pattern of short and long syllables carefully arranged into feet and lines and stanzas. Instead, to use Fulke Greville's characterization of the *Arcadia*, the aim of a poet is 'to turn the barren Philosophy precepts into pregnant Images of life.'[12]

NOTES

1. I am using 'political' here in its literal sense,

derived from πόλις, *city*, and therefore equivalent to 'social.'

2. What I call the neoplatonic esthetic is laid out by Landino in prefatory essays to his edition of Dante, *Divina commedia* (Florence, 1481), *8v-*10. Sidney mentions Landino in connection with Dante (*Misc. Prose*, 121.15-25). Sidney knew Landino's essay 'Divino furore' probably from Francesco Sansovino's edition of *Dante con l'espositione di Cristoforo Landino, et di Allesandro Vellutello, sopra la sua Comedia dell'Inferno, del Purgatorio, & del Paradiso* (Venice, 1564), with a second edition at Venice, 1578.

3. Dryden says: 'I have called my poem *historical*, not *epic*, though both the actions and actors are so much heroic as any poem can contain' (*Essays*, ed. W.P. Ker [2 vols., Oxford, 1900]), I.ii).

4. Plutarch, *The morals*, tr. Philemon Holland (London, 1603), p. 983.

5. See Leon Battista Alberti, *On Painting and On Sculpture*, tr. Cecil Grayson (London, 1972), pp. 73-85.

6. See Cicero, *Tusculanarum disputationes*, V.xxxix.114. Cf. Lucian, *Icones*, 8.

7. Philostratus, *Imagines* et al., tr. Arthur Fairbanks (London, 1969), p. 3.

8. Aristotle, *Rhetorica*, 1411b: Quintilian, *Institutio oratoria*, VIII.iii.61-2: Thomas Wilson, *The arte of rhetorique* (London, 1553), fol. 104-104v.

9. See *De oratore*, III.163.

10. *'Copia': Foundations of the Abundant Style*, tr. Betty I. Knott, in *Collected Works of Erasmus*, ed. Craig R. Thompson (24 vols., Toronto, 1974-), XXIV.577.

11. 117.9. Sidney spells the word ἐνέργεια, the term used by Aristotle in the *Rhetoric*. By Sidney's day, however, the terms ἐνέργεια and ἐνάργεια had become inextricably confused; cf. George Puttenham, *The Arte of English Poesie*, ed. Gladys D. Willcock and Alice Walker (Cambridge, 1963), pp. 142-3.

12. *Life of Sir Philip Sidney* [1652], ed. Nowell Smith (Oxford, 1907), p. 15.

THE MEETING OF THE MUSES: SIDNEY AND THE MID-TUDOR POETS

Germaine Warkentin

Let us consider a certain collection of Elizabethan lyrics, a lengthy series of poems in various forms, and uttered by a first person speaker. It presents us with the irrational passion of the poet for a woman he can never attain. His beloved is a paragon of virtue, whom he nevertheless accuses of being a tiger's child; watching her embark on the Thames he is overcome with the effects of her beauty. On another occasion he reproves his tongue for not having spoken out when she was free; now alas she is ill-matched with another. In an attempt to console the poet, the lady explains how her lover should conduct himself. I am speaking, of course, of George Turbervile's so-called 'Pyndara and Tymetes' collection of 1563-67, and we are concerned with it because of the uncommon resemblance of the features I have just itemized to Philip Sidney's *Astrophil and Stella*, written nearly two decades later.[1]

I am certainly not going to spend time 'proving' that *Astrophil and Stella* was derived from 'Pyndara and Tymetes'; nevertheless, we should consider what is implied by the existence of those parallels. Indeed, several poems of the same sort (for example the one in which the lover reproves himself for not speaking) crop up as well in Barnabe Googe's *Eglogs Epytaphes and Sonettes* of 1563.[2] In the 'digression on England' of his *Defence of Poetry* Sidney finds little to praise in the English poets of his own age, though his view of the future of English lyric is more hopeful. He names few of his contemporaries, and seems rather to pursue with them the same strategy he adopts in the *Defence* as a whole, which is to rebut Gosson while ignoring him. Yet the parallels I cited above suggest at the very least that Sidney was willing to engage here and there with the *topoi* of contemporary lyric poetry, if only to show--as he certainly did--how much better he could carry them off. Stella's heart, you will recall, is of *no* tiger's kind.

But I propose to argue for more than that 'very least' in this paper. Yvor Winters--in an article actually very

hostile to Sidney's influence on Elizabethan poetry--once
reminded us that Sidney and Spenser were in an important sense
transitional figures, bridging the sobriety of style and purpose Winters admired in the mid-Tudor poets and the sensuous,
ironic, highly decorated strain he deplored in their Petrarchan successors.[3] Unlike Spenser, Sidney did not survive to
write poetry in the golden nineties, so we do well, now and
again, to close our ears to that later music and consider him
as one of the heirs of Tottel. I will do so in order to make
two points. One is that though Sidney may have looked down
on lyricists of the sixties and seventies, he clearly read
them very attentively. The second is that in doing so he
absorbed a way of envisioning the poet-lover's experience--
a way 'full, material, and circumstantiated' as Lamb memorably described it[4]--which had an important creative effect
on the manifest Petrarchism of *Astrophil and Stella*.

My chosen perspective is not, however, that offered by
the esthetics of the individual poem, but by the architecture
of whole collections, which is where, in the case of the
sonnet sequence, what one might call the *locus* of creativity
equally lies. The romantic and modern concentration on the
single poem does not serve us well as a way of looking at
poems produced by rhetorical methods of composition like
those practiced before the eighteenth century. In such poems
the exploitation of established *topoi*--as well as their persistent inversion--produces a dense network of common allusions which links together poems good and bad from many
languages and from two millenia. The Thames voyage undertaken by Pyndara and later by Stella has its origin in poem
225 of Petrarch's *Canzoniere*, a vision of Laura in a boat
upon the waves (probably of the Rhone). And astonishingly,
it seems at least possible that poems like Sidney's four
sonnets on the lady's toothache in *Certain Sonnets*, or on
Stella's sickness (101 and 102, and probably 100 as well)
have their inception in some earlier poet's need to turn to
acceptable purpose the commiserating stance of Ovid when, in
Amores II, xiii and xiv, he confronts the effects of Corin-
na's self-induced abortion. This method of composition tends
to make each poem an individual variation on a set theme, a
theme which in its turn distills the collected images of an
entire tradition of culture. Faced by such a daunting set
of cross-references, we might be reduced to mere classifica-
tion, were it not that in the sonnet sequence or canzoniere--
itself a highly conventionalized genre--we can turn to the
way in which poem is related to poem in a given collection to
find out how the poet's imagination is working. It is in
such relationships--schematic and rhetorical ones, rather
than the thematic ones we are used to perceiving--that we
will discover how Sidney could share a substantial number of
topoi with, say, Turbervile, reject outright the direction
in which Turbervile is led by them, and yet at the same time

subtly draw upon the example of the rejected collection.

Rejection, of course, is part of the legacy of design with which Petrarch's contention with Dante endowed the sonnet sequence. Exploiting elements drawn both from the Boethian *consolatio* and the Provencal *chansonnier*, Dante in his *Vita Nuova* had synthesized a new kind of work: a collection of lyrics with attached commentary in which the poet, speaking in the first person, presents himself both as maker or *auctor* of his book, and as the *materia* of the book itself. In such a work the poet, in an examination of his inward experience of love, reaches some new kind of knowledge and at the same time demonstrates his valour in art. Its design is determined by the significance he attaches to the character of that inward experience, to its status as text, and to his position as *auctor* within the greater text of God's creation. In Dante's case the design takes a highly schematic form, in which balanced numbers of sonnets and canzoni are arranged in a pyramid, the apex of which is an important canzone. Yet this schematic pattern also provides a simple narrative thread, by which the lover moves from confusion to a reordered state of mind in the manner of the consolatio. The result is the book Dante calls a *libello*: something small, expressive of personal rather than public feeling, and constituting a miniature analogue of the *libro*, the book of creation in which, the *Commedia* assures us, is gathered in one great volume that which in human existence is scattered in separate leaves throughout the universe.[5]

Petrarch's version of this new kind of work is fuelled by a fierce rivalry with his eminent predecessor, as well as by a return to the classics, to Ovid and Propertius. Thus in his *Canzoniere* we do not have the 'planet like music' of Dante's pyramidal schema, but the *rime sparse*--scattered rhymes--of an arrangement according to the classical principle of *variatio*, and chosen to express Petrarch's conviction that such variety was a medical symptom of the hapless human malady of love.[6] There is no sure movement of the lover towards 'nova intelligenza,' but rather his desperate attempt to make sense out of a fragmented truth, not the confident *lectio* provided by Dante's commented poems, but the fevered question, 'alas, which poem comes last, and which comes first?' (*Canz.* 127:4). Shaped into a calendrical structure, yet constantly denying it, Petrarch's *Canzoniere* presents the reader not with a model of creation, but with a simulacrum of the poet's psyche confined to the perimeters of its own consciousness, and thus to his uniquely human nature. With this goes a rhetorical method in which the vision of the *rime sparse* and the language of a disrupted *lectio* are united in the persistent exploration of the contraries of human experience, a method in which poem is linked to poem by controlled amplifications and inversions, rather than by the explanatory drive of a narrative line or the reassuring completeness of an ornamental, schematized design.

The myriad sonnet sequences and canzonieri which constitute the late-Renaissance *libello* reflect these contrasts. In one version of the *libello* there is a Dantesque confidence in the poet's orderly emergence from his suffering into an intelligible cosmos, a confidence which expresses itself either in the quasi-narrative pattern of the *consolatio* tradition, or in balanced, schematized design, or both. The other, and much more prevalent, Petrarchan design insists that the poet is primarily a natural being, who can contemplate—though ironically never achieve—transcendence.[7] The attractiveness of such a vision to the searching minds of the Renaissance is obvious; what is less obvious is its influence as a purely compositional model. Petrarch's *Canzoniere* presented its audience with a method of reading which persistently frustrates the reader as it insists on the doubtfulness of the text being assembled. This effect was early aggravated by the editorial problem resulting from the *Canzoniere*'s transmission in manuscripts in which the order of the poems was frequently variant. The consequence of this multiplex fragmentation was to turn the *Canzoniere* into a common-place book, one in which all that could be said about love was assembled ready for the apprentice to unpack. The contraries Petrarch had seen in the human condition were transposed, in most cases, from the visionary to the rhetorical plane, and the opportunities they afforded for praise and blame, combined with Petrarch's own allusiveness and rhetoricism, turned the *Canzoniere* into a school of eloquence for Renaissance vernacular lyricists. The making of such a collection involved not merely commitment to a particular literary genre, but the adoption of a special and peculiarly self-demonstrating role, one which centred on the poet's constant public analysis of his own creativity.

It is generally assumed that this version of the canzoniere was introduced into England by Sidney and Watson in the 1580s. Yet mid-Tudor poets knew the *libello* well, perhaps because in the early sixties the Inns of Court from which that essentially bourgeois and academic group emerged were full of Marian exiles who had had ample contact with the continental literature. In their employment of it, however, they maintained an austere distance from the Petrarchizing of their continental contemporaries, for the moral stance of the second generation of Tudor humanists stressed the civic over the speculative, the ethical over the psychological.[8] They had, furthermore, an unfeignedly nativist program for English poetry, one they could pursue because they had their own common-place book to stand duty for Petrarch: *Tottel's Miscellany* (1557), which provided the models for individual lyrics in the more than a dozen 'gentleman's miscellanies' published between 1563 and the mid-1580s. The influence of Tottel notwithstanding, these volumes attest to the mid-Tudor poet's clear grasp of the central principle of the *libello*: that a book of lyrics in the first person, set in order by the author himself, might exemplify his vision of his own creativity.

The mid-Tudor *libello* was not the rhetorically flexible, metaphorically fertile canzoniere, but something closer to the medieval *speculum morale*. In Turbervile's words it was intended both to 'pleasure and recreate thy wearye mind and troubled hed withal' (TI, f. *5^r) and to warn 'all tender age to flee that fonde and filthie affection of poysoned & unlawful love. Let this be a Glasse & Myrror for them to gaze upon' (TI, f. *6^{r-v}). Like Petrarch, mid-Tudor poets relied on the unhappy medical condition of the lover, with his disoriented perceptions and alternating fever and chills, to explain the loose arrangement of collections the order of which was frequently revised from edition to edition. Yet the image of the glass, the *speculum* stabilized their collections conceptually at least, and prevented them from rendering fully the Petrarchan theme of the doubtful text; when Turbervile expresses disgust with his 'booke of barren verse and vaine' (TII, f. 196^v) it is because the ethical model of such works is so very clear to him, not because like Astrophil he is saying 'thus write I while I doubt to write' (*Astrophil and Stella*, 34). In his verse-preface to Googe's volume, L. Blundeston calls this experience of continuity-within-discontinuity the 'long reherse of tryed fayth by tyme' (f.Biii^r), and all the gentleman's miscellanies pay lip-service to it. We might attribute this to the subterranean working of Petrarch's 'molti e molti anni' (*Canz.* 332:55), so productive of sheer *copia* in Italian collections, were it not that the compositional result is very much a poetry of statement: that kind of poetry Leonard Nathan calls 'categorical.'[9] Despite its resourceful employment of rhetorical *contraria*, the goal of such poetry is not the dialectical exploration of the inner life of the natural man, but the defining and ordering of the poet's experience in accordance with publicly accepted norms. Its representative poems are not the sonnet or the literary song (the *canzone*), but the catalogue, the aphoristic poem of moral advice, the musical song, the epitaph.

Thus the mid-Tudor poet compiling a gentleman's miscellany has, without realizing it, a complex problem of design. He has adopted the formalized randomness of the Petrarchan canzoniere, and assumed certain features of its *mythos* of the frenzied poet-lover, yet his rhetorical objectives and his *mentalité* urge him towards the public poem and the intelligible cosmos. We can see the results in designs employed by the three most important poets who used the *libello* before Sidney, designs which for reasons of time I must sketch in a very simplified form. Barnabe Googe's solution is fundamentally schematic. His volume is first divided by genre into the 'eglogs,' 'epytaphes,' and 'sonettes' of its title. The first two sections preserve the generic consistency proclaimed by their headings; the 'sonettes,' on the other hand, appear to be very miscellaneous. Or at least they seem so, until we realize that many of the poems are in fact contrasted varia-

21

tions on set themes, and that our eye is being drawn to
Googe's display of this ability to vary, to produce *copia*, by
two formal units which, taken together, compose a frame: the
four verse portraits of exemplary figures at the beginning,
and the dream vision, 'Cupido Conquered,' at the end. Googe's
collection, in other words, is markedly formal but not in any
way thematic.

An interest in rhetorical display for its own sake is
very marked in Turbervile's two collections. But the design
of the first of these, the *Epitaphes, Epigrams, Songs and
Sonets* (perhaps as early as 1563, but published as already
revised in the first known edition, of 1567), shows that in
addition he has perceived the relationship in Petrarch's
Canzoniere between the work's formal variety and its central
subject, the moral disruption of the lover. The title fore-
casts a generic collection like Googe's, but in reality the
forms of the poems are mixed. Ignoring refinements of detail
such as the formal opening sonnet of the continental canzoniere, Turbervile isolates and adapts its quasi-narrative
features, even to giving names to his lover and lady as Sidney
later does: they are 'Pyndara' (fairly clearly identified
with the book's dedicatee, Anne, Countess of Warwick) and
'Tymetes' (the author of the poems).[10] It is not clear how
either of them dealt with the problems involved in manifestly
identifying a patroness both with Pandora and, as later poems
make clear, Criseyde. Tymetes' passion shows the familiar
alternating pattern of *varietas*:

> Thus twixt dispaire and hope the doubtfull man
> Long space did live that loved *Pyndara*,

and as with Petrarch, and later Astrophil, his love gives rise
to poetry:

> . . . ever as *Tymetes* had the cause
> Of ioy or smart, of comfort or refuse:
> He glad or griefull woxe, and ever drawes
> His present state with Pen as here ensues.
>
> (TI, f. 3^v)

Elsewhere Turbervile did not feel himself confined to the example of the Petrarchan *libello* alone; his second collection
(probably from the mid-1570s) belongs to the same sub-genre
of the canzoniere as Du Bellay's *Regrets* and *Antiquitez de
Rome*; there a virtually unmediated first-person voice presents the juxtaposed experiences of travel to Russia (which
he visited as part of a diplomatic mission in 1568-69), and
the consequent, and complicating, separation from a beloved.
The architectonic instinct Turbervile displays in attempting
two distinct versions of the *libello* is unhappily not matched
with any verbal gifts or visionary insight. He is the most

dully rhetorical of poets, and the frequency with which Sidney exploits elements of the canzoniere which Turbervile had fumbled suggests to me that he had read 'Pyndara and Tymetes' with active disdain.

The 'Devises' contained in George Gascoigne's *A Hundreth sundrie Flowres* (1573, revised 1575)[11] compose a collection more brilliant than any before Sidney's, both in their rhetorical and structural fertility and in Gascoigne's mastery of the speaking voice, a mastery which poets of the next two decades were also to seek in their own ways. The contrast between the two versions is extremely illuminating. Both are made up of almost exactly the same poems; in 1573 they are described as the poems of 'sundry gentlemen,' and are presented by the commenting voice of the original version of *The Adventures of Master F.J.* (who calls himself 'G.T.') as an appendage to that work. But both the diverse subgroups of poems and their rambunctious prose head-notes are clearly by Gascoigne, here ranging beyond mere verbal *copia* to produce a copious flood of *personae*. (Like Sidney's 'I am not I, pitie the tale of me,' this is simply a way of toying with the difference between a poetic mask and the unmediated first person conventional to the canzoniere.) The transformation Gascoigne worked on the same poems in his revision of 1575 shows the direction in which the English *libello* was preparing to move: 'G.T.' disappears as a commenting voice, and the poems of the various 'gentlemen,' now dispersed in three groups, are all treated as if they were the work of a single hand. Their voice is identified in three formal prefatory letters to the book as a whole with the poet himself, who speaks as if he is now finished with the excesses of youth and is ready to appear as a man of age and experience. The arrangement of the poems exemplifies this new and perhaps mockingly elaborate pose of sobriety, for the three groups have been decorously worked into a schematized design of 'Flowers' (to recreate), 'Hearbes' (to cure), and 'Weedes' (to serve as negative *exempla*).

In each of these poets, the disordered psychology of the lover has its rhetorical expression, as it does in Petrarch, yet all of them exhibit the desire to control this *varietas*, whether through external ordering devices, as with Googe, through the exploitation of dimly-perceived structural exemplars, as with Turbervile, or by means of diagrammatic play with the resources of voice, as with Gascoigne. That this need for control gained in importance as they experimented with the *libello* is suggested by Gascoigne's settling on a schematic arrangement in revising *A Hundreth sundrie Flowres*. Associated with it is the sober and outward-looking stance to which all these poets were drawn, a stance exemplified in Googe's portraits of virtuous men and the moral cast of 'Cupido Conquered,' in Turbervile's heavy-handed struggle with the problem of writing about virtue, and in Gascoigne's self-conscious adoption of the wise mask of the aging poet (he was about 33 in 1575). Whatever their differences, all three poets share a common moral language, a language found as well in the minor gentleman's miscellanies of the same decades, miscellanies which lack their structural sophistication.

Three elements of supreme importance to Sidney emerge from the gentleman's miscellanies considered as a group. First, is the persistence through all of them of that ethical perspective we have seen, one public and civic in its orientation rather than private and psychological; the identity and social role of the poem are always established and validated by the poems of moral advice he exchanges with other gentleman poets, whose answers are printed with his own. Sidney exchanges poems once in *Certain Sonnets*; thereafter he dramatizes the same kind of material, and the result is poems like *Astrophil and Stella*, 21, 'Your words, my friend (right healthfull caustiks) blame/My young mind marde,' which a reader of the 80s would have seen as belonging to a very familiar mode.

Second is the special role played by women. The continental canzoniere in its purest form excludes poems employing the voice of the mistress, though many such poems were written and appear in more miscellaneous collections; the voice of the *libello* is uniquely--indeed, necessarily--that of the lover who creates it. But in the mid-Tudor collections women are frequently permitted to utter their own laments: 'An absent Dame thus complayneth,' writes Gascoigne (GI, p. 320), and Turbervile presents 'A gentlewoman's excuse for executing unlawfull partes of love' (TII, f.195^v). Not frequently there recurs the motif of the woman who has married someone unworthy of her (in one or two places he is specifically referred to as a miser). Even more important is the guise of the unworthy woman in which the beloved sometimes appears, reminding us of the profound influence of Chaucer's Criseyde on the poets of the age, whether like Googe and Turbervile they refer to her directly, or whether as with Gabriel Harvey later on, *Troilus and Criseyde* is assumed to have been 'one of Astrophil's cordials.'[12] In the absence of the kind of intellectualized secular idealism practiced by continental neoplatonists, this native theme assumes real importance; here we see the ancestry in part of Greville's cynical Caelica, of the prudent Stella who bids Astrophil, 'Peace, I thinke that some give eare:/Come no more, least I get anger,' of Spenser's jeering Rosalind, 'the Widdowes daughter of the glenne,' and of the Dark Lady of Shakespeare's *Sonnets*.

Third, there is the peculiarly circumstantial texture of these works, which deeply affects both their use of the first person and the linkage of poem to poem. In the archetype of the continental canzoniere, Petrarch's insistence on the identity between the fictive Petrarch of the poems and the real Petrarch who wrote them is at one and the same time a statement of fact and the exploitation of an emerging convention;[13] Dante before him had done so, mingling the elements of personal testimony in the *consolatio* tradition (newly emergent also in contemporary vernacular lyric) with his characteristically intense awareness of the rich historicity of Divine creation. And of course there is the Ovidian precedent with which Petrarch plays so deftly. 'This, too, is the work of my pen,' as Ovid writes in *Amores* II, i, 'mine, Naso's, born among the humid Paeligni, the well-known singer of my own worthless ways.' For the mid-Tudor poet, this interest in what Paul Zumthor calls 'I-discourse'[14]--the capacity of the self to state its own reality--is strengthened by the highly-evolved tradition of unmediated first-person discourse which comes to him from the English dream-vision, where he would have met a type of poem in which a first-person speaker narrates his experience of a world which is fictive, because it is a dream, yet at the same time real, because it is *his* dream. Such poems draw on the same Boethian sources exploited by Dante, and on the same historicist assumptions: the dreamer enters his dream in a state of moral disruption, and in a continuous examination of conscience, often undertaken with the help of an interlocutor, effects a cure which is expected to have consequences for his life outside the dream. There is at least one work in the prehistory of the English sonnet sequence--Cavendish's *Metrical Visions* of 1552--which is a group of shorter poems drawn together by the authority of a single first person speaker who is just such a dreamer.

In the mid-Tudor *libello* it is part of the poet's assertion of the intelligibility of the cosmos that though his experience may have merely hypothetical status, he himself stands as a historical reference point behind the experience he relates. If Turbervile 'by meere fiction of these Fantasies' forewarns his youthful readers of the dangers of base love, he at the same time drives his point home by asserting that the speaking voice of the poems inhabits the same experiential world as the reader of them: 'the soner may I (I trust) prevayle in my persuasiō, for that my selfe am of their yeares and disposition' (TI, f*6^{r-v}). A first consequence of this is the implicit assumption of these works that the suffering lover's advice will have its effect, his example prevail, his self-examination induce in him some new condition of being. And this acceptance of process and change brings with it the possibility, still latent and unrealized, of sequential narrative. A second consequence is that the mid-Tudor poet is committed to a concept of poetic voice which is relatively naive according to modernist theory, but which by its very nature is richly circumstantial. I am aware of the unpopularity of this view, but before you dismiss it as the kind of naive euhaemerism that used to insist that in sonnet sequences poets 'unlocked their hearts,' I urge you to consider the instance of Herbert's examination of conscience in his devotional canzoniere, *The Temple*, an examination which would be without spiritual meaning if art and life were not connected in some important way for the poet.

The compiling of Sidney's *Certain Sonnets* was, I contend, undertaken within the parameters established by such collections. Yet Sidney's critique of them is clear, both in the elements he selected to hypertrophy and in those he seems to have ignored. *Certain Sonnets* shows its connection with the gentleman's miscellany in a number of superficial ways: the exchange of poems, the songs 'to the tune of . . . ,' the fact that like several of them it is attached to a larger work (the *Arcadia*),15 and in particular in its uneven decorum, the 'diseguaglianza di livello e di tono poetico' marked by Vanna Gentili.16 And of course its two famous concluding sonnets, the sombreness of which partly causes this imbalance, are drawn straight from the mid-Tudor ethical mode. In *Certain Sonnets* Sidney, like other poets of the seventies, is using Tottel for his commonplace book; he is still employing the catalogue, the obvious verbal schema, the musical song, the classical allusion, the poem of moral advice. All of these forms are shaped by his evident taste and poetic intelligence, but they represent not a movement away from Tottel's modes, but a perfecting of them.

At the same time as we recognize this, however, we can see the forms of another poetic emerging. Sidney, for his songs, has gone to school to Montemayor as well as Tottel, and he is much more interested in the sonnet and its possibilities for rhetorical variation than the mid-Tudors were. He opens his collection, for example, with a Petrarchan *excusatio* and *innamoramento*, the first in English. And the set of sonnets 'made when his Ladie had paine in her face' rhetorically varies the poet's topic to the point where the resources of mid-Tudor poetry are strained to the breaking-point. Sidney's struggle with this new poetic is interestingly reflected in the design of *Certain Sonnets*. No poet of the seventies came to the *libello* with anything like his experience in the design of groups of short poems, experience which he gained in working out the complex pattern of the *Arcadia* eclogues. Nor did anyone else have his experience in the exploitation of dramatic voice, for all those poems had been written in the first person. Their voices were, however, the voices of different people, fictive personalities from which Sidney could distance himself. The problem posed by the gentleman's miscellany was the need to exploit a single voice throughout a varied collection, and furthermore, if what I have argued holds true, to validate that voice by reference to the poet's personal experience. This task Sidney specifically refuses. Indeed, in *Certain Sonnets* he refuses the circumstantial, the experienced world almost entirely. Apart from the exchange with Dyer and one personal reference in *Certain Sonnets* 22, the scene of the poems is not the public and academic one of the gentleman's miscellanies, nor even Petrarch's *vallis clausa*, populous with imagined presences, but the heremtically sealed world of a solitary poet lost in song. So enclosed is this world that the plaintive gentlewoman of the mid-Tudor collections is excluded from it, and the poet's assiduous correspondents (with one exception) as well. It is as if Sidney had to conduct an autopsy on the *libello*, stripping away what he could not immediately use, in order to master its essentials on his own terms.

The plan of *Certain Sonnets* in the version printed in the 1598 folio reflects the disdain for the mid-Tudor *Libello* which required Sidney to do this, while at the same time ironically remaining within its boundaries. In column I of the diagram (see Figure 1), I have tried to lay out one aspect of the collection's design: the disposition of poems by type and *topos* which makers of canzoniere habitually played with, sometimes matching poems in elegant schemas (as Sidney does with *Certain Sonnets* 3 - 7 and 23 - 27), sometimes grouping related poems together (*Certain Sonnets* 8 - 11, on a common topic, *Certain Sonnets* 12 - 14, translations from Latin, *Certain Sonnets* 23 and 29 from Montemayor), sometimes varying the arrangement irregularly (*Certain Sonnets* 15 - 22, where, furthermore, the first and last poems frame the others with major allusions to neighbouring poems in Petrarch). Sidney has used all these devices in the same short canzoniere, balancing form against form, mode against mode, to make the elegant, schematized, and context-less 'device' which is the appropriate expression of the solitary voice of the poem. Preoccupied with thematic and narrative ways of reading, we have lost the capacity to perceive such patterns, which is why *Certain Sonnets* has almost uniformly been described as without shape, too loose and miscellaneous to be a true collection.[17] A true collection it is, but one in which Sidney distances himself fiercely from contemporary influences, while at the same time in his play with rough symmetries, unwittingly reflecting them. Rewarding though these poems can be, we are still some distance from *Astrophil and Stella*.

I have argued elsewhere at length and in complex detail what I regard as the codicological grounds for believing that the Bodleian manuscript (e Museo 37) represents Sidney's effort, typical among the compilers of such miscellanies, to tear down this structure and reassemble it on different lines.[18] Here I must present that proposition simply as a working hypothesis. In column II of the diagram can be seen what I think Sidney did. The most obvious feature of the new arrangement is that all those poems which aided the purely schematic design of what I call the original version of *Certain Sonnets* are separated from the 'varied' poems and set to

The Meeting of the Muses

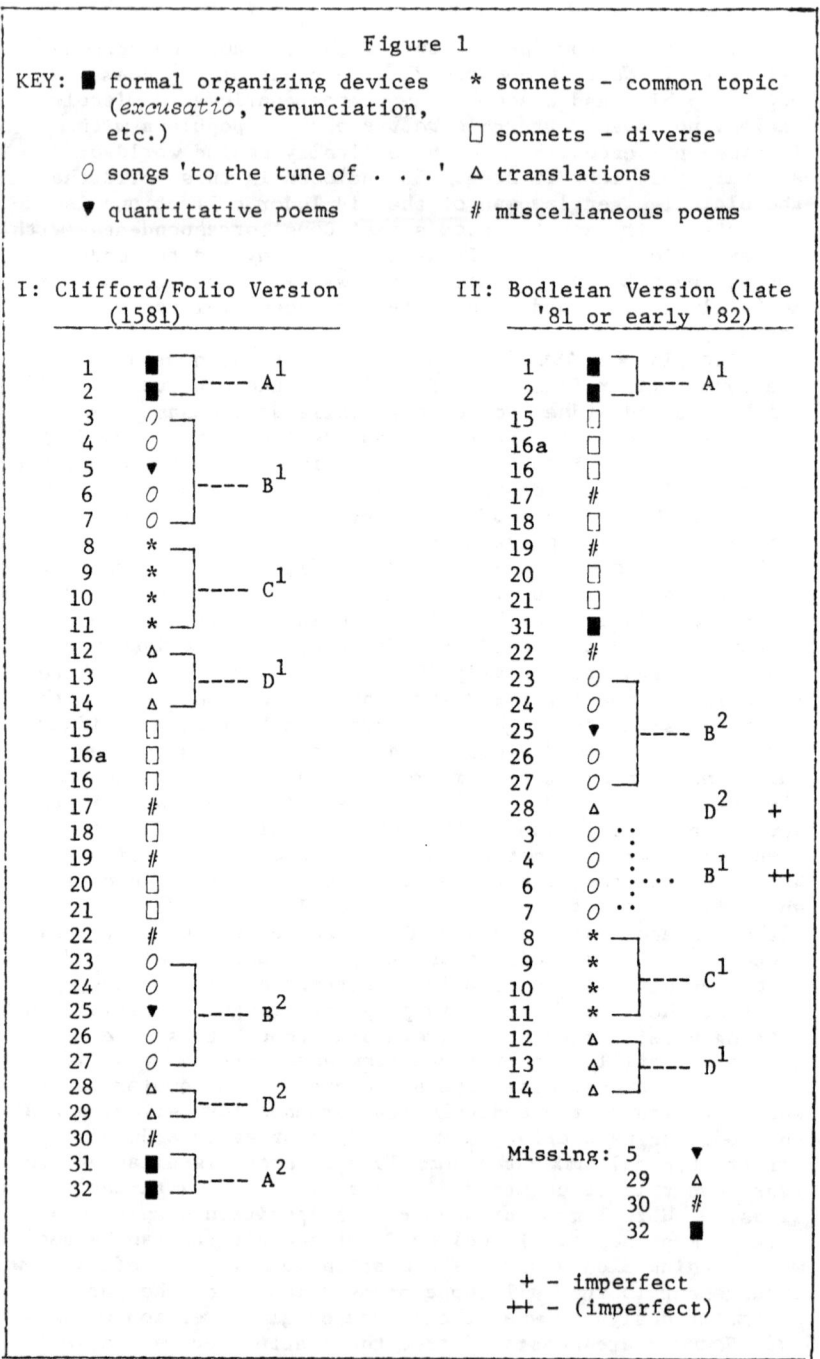

one side; these are the lyrics typical of the gentleman's miscellany, but not of the canzoniere, and it is interesting that Sidney's decision to separate them from the others goes far to resolve the problem of decorum noted by Gentili. A second result is that the 'varied' poems, freed of their schematized frame, are held together by nothing but the fact that they are uttered by a single voice, and with this isolation of the voice of the poems comes a focussing on the situation in which they are placed by the Petrarchan *excusatio* and *innamoramento* which still begin the collection. I have no idea which effect Sidney was seeking--a more refined decorum, or a more intensely focussed voice--but both play a large part in the achievement of *Astrophil and Stella*. In addition to this, however, we can recognize another shift, one taking place at a deeper level of structure. The nearly symmetrical tripartite schema of the first version of *Certain Sonnets* visibly expresses the ideal aims of poetry as Sidney defended them in his great treatise; it is a 'sovereign' device, of the same complex type as that which, to a very different purpose, organizes 'Yee Gote-heard Gods.' In the second version this balance and symmetry disappears, and the design collapses into a feeble dichotomy. But this collapse is potentially very fruitful; out of it Sidney will be able to build the looser and more ironic structure he gives to Astrophil's conflicts. For it was to write *Astrophil and Stella* that he now abandoned, it seems, this redrafted but inconclusive design.

    I have left *Astrophil and Stella* for a few last remarks because the things I want to say about it at this point are so large and simple. They also return us to Lamb's historic response to the sequence, which despite our various and conflicting approaches remains the critical consensus on that power to move the reader which--*pace* Yvor Winters--Sidney has, and Turbervile does not. The Tudor poetic voice is constrained by the very orderliness of its vision. Its best poets find escape from this orderliness difficult; Wyatt and Surrey seek a way out through the genre and stance of complaint, Skelton and later Gascoigne in a wild, uncentred mischievousness. Sidney's escape is by the fiercely intelligent, but costly, route of irony, an irony which is the verbal counterpart of the structural irony Spenser had discovered in *The Shepheardes Calender*. It was from the Petrarchan canzoniere that Sidney learned the psychology, the virtually neoplatonic forms of idealization, and the meta-poetic stance of the school of eloquence which European poetry for two centuries had attended. And it was there he also learned, like a horseman in the ring returning again and again to the figures of the *manège*, the disciplines of a rhetoric which would make possible a truly dialectical, and fully ironic poetry, with all the visionary risks such poetry entails. Freighted with this cargo, *Astrophil and Stella* emerges as the first true Petrarchan canzoniere in English literature.

The Meeting of the Muses

It does so with a difference, however, one for which the mid-Tudor *libello* is accountable. *Astrophil and Stella* (for complex reasons not always consequent on the poetics of the seventies) shows signs of Sidney's continued interest in formal schematization. James Cotter, Alastair Fowler, and Thomas P. Roche, Jr., have variously pointed to the 'sovereign' position of the songs, and to the significance of the numbers 108 and 63.[19] However, in *Astrophil and Stella* these schemas are not an end in themselves, but a means to an end: to give shape to Sidney's voicing of another kind of vision entirely, one which ruptures the firmly conceived moral universe of the mid-Tudor *libello* and plunges poet and reader into the conditional and problematic. The resources for this plunge Sidney finds, in part, in the mid-Tudor *libello*. From it he draws his portrait of Stella; Petrarchan mistress she is, but at the same time the lamenting gentlewoman of many a Tudor poem; the fairest book of nature, yet also the pragmatic lady who sternly closes the window on her beseeching suitor. It is out of the mid-Tudor *libello*'s alliance with the dream-vision that Sidney forges the union of personal immediacy and narrative strength that reshapes utterly the English reader's perception of the resources of the Italian *rime sparse*. Then, finally, there is the moral stance of the poems, in which the battle of reason and passion is shaped by the specifically civic ideals Astrophil knows he ought to be fulfilling, but cannot. Here Sidney draws repeatedly on the moral language of Googe, Turbervile, Howell, and the others, as is revealed by a close comparison between Googe's 'To M. Edwarde Cobham' and *Astrophil and Stella 5*, to take only one example. Furthermore, he exacts from this civic mode the widest range of visionary possibilities, situating its values both in the circumstantial world of Philip Sidney, whose father half-tamed Ulster with his golden bit, and equally among the purely ethical images of that landscape of the 'heroicke mind' which is lit only by an inward sun.

Ben Jonson, surveying another landscape several decades later, marked at Penshurst,

> That taller tree, which of a nut was set
> At his great birth, where all the muses met.
> ('To Penshusrt,' 13-14)

What I have said here is intended to provide a new perspective on that meeting of the muses. Yet--and this is my final contention--Sidney's debt to mid-Tudor poetry is something we have always subconsciously heeded. The sign of that subconscious acquiescence--fittingly, in view of our shape-changing poet--is in one of the jokes of the Sidnaeian editorial and critical tradition: Sonnets '109' and '110' of *Astrophil and Stella*. Despite all the textual evidence to the contrary, we long to submit, as even David Kalstone acknowledges, to the delusion that *Certain Sonnets* 31 and 32 form the appropriate ending to *Astrophil and Stella*.[20] The reason is that they are the fullest expression in either of Sidney's collections of the ethos of the gentleman's miscellany, and that ethos is an important presence in *Astrophil and Stella*. Their sternness and sobriety make them grotesquely inappropriate to the songbook of the solitary singer, but they fall into their real place in the complex personal drama of Astrophil, which is ethically more polarized and at the same time more persuasively circumstantial. Though in Sonnet 108 Sidney brings *Astrophil and Stella* to a standstill in the 'joy/annoy' stasis of the continental tradition, in Sonnet 107 he provides us with a reworking of those two earlier farewells to love, a reworking in which the values of the mid-Tudor *libello* are transmuted at last into an image where real and ideal can actively engage with each other: the image of the heroic task. It was that subject, of course, which was to dominate the last major work which Sidney wrote.

NOTES

1. George Turbervile, *Epitaphes, Epigrams, Songs and Sonets* (1567) and *Epitaphes and Sonnettes* (1576). Facsimile, introduction by Richard J. Panofsky (Delmar, N.Y., 1977). Referred to in my text as TI (the earlier collection) and TII (the later). Page numbers are those of the original in facsimile, not the modern pagination added to the facsimile text. The examples given are as follows: 'tiger's child' TI, f.116^v; 'Thames' TI, f.18^r; 'reproves his tongue' TI, f.101^v; 'ill-matched with another' TI, f.117^r; 'mutual consolation' TI, f21^r and 24^r. Panofsky calls the sequence 'Pyndara and Tymetes,' which is not strictly correct, but eminently practical, given the volume's title as published.

2. Barnabe Googe, *Eglogs Epytaphes and Sonettes*. London, 1563. Compare with the examples in note 1: 'Maystresse A.' is accused of having a tiger's heart on f. Fvii^v, and 'Unhappye tonge, why dydste thou not consent,' f. Gv^v.

3. Winters' influential essay 'The 16th Century Lyric in England' was published in parts in *Poetry (Chicago)*, v. 53 and v. 54 (1939); revised, it appeared in *Forms of Discovery: Critical and Historical Essays on the Forms of the Short Poem in English* (Denver, 1967), pp. 1-120.

4. Charles Lamb, 'Some Sonnets of Sir Philip Sydney,' in *Last Essays of Elia* (London, 1833), p. 149.

5. See Piero Boitani, 'The Sybil's Leaves: A Study of *Paradiso XXXIII*,' *Dante Studies*, 96 (1978), pp. 83-147, and note 6 below.

6. In 1373 Petrarch sent a copy of his *Canzoniere* to Pandolfo Malatesta with the observation that the variety of these little works in the vernacular was to be explained by the 'instabilis furor amantium' which was treated at the beginning, that is, in the first poem (*Variae*, ix). Robert M. Durling drew attention to this correspondence between medical

pathology and literary form in *The Figure of the Poet in Renaissance Epic* (Cambridge, Mass., 1965), p. 86. Implications of the esthetic of *varietas* which are taken for granted in this essay I have tried to argue more fully elsewhere; see Germaine Warkentin '"Love's sweetest part, variety": Petrarch and the Curious Frame of the Renaissance Sonnet Sequence,' *Renaissance and Reformation*, 11 (1975), pp. 14-23; 'The Form of Dante's 'Libello' and its Challenge to Petrarch,' *Quaderni d'italianistica* II (1981), pp. 160-70; 'Sidney and the Supple Muse: Compositional Procedures in Some Sonnets of *Astrophil and Stella*,' *SLit I* 15 (1982), pp. 37-48.

7. Two good contrasting examples are by the neoplatonist Jacques Peletier du Mans, *L'Amour des Amours* (1555), and Pierre de Ronsard, *Sonets pour Hélène* (1578).

8. For the ethos of these poets, and its relation to stylistic problems which cannot be treated here, see especially G.K. Hunter, 'Drab and Golden Lyrics of the Renaissance,' in *Forms of Lyric: Selected Papers from the English Institute*, ed. Reuben Brower (New York, 1970), pp. 1-18, and Richard J. Panofsky, '"And All Their Talke and Studie is Of It": The Problem of Amatory Content in Earlier Elizabethan Polite Verse,' forthcoming in *Studies in Philology*. See also the essays in Sloan and Waddington, note 9, below.

9. Leonard Nathan, 'Gascoigne's 'Lullabie' and Structures in the Tudor Lyric,' in Thomas O. Sloan and Raymond B. Waddington, *The Rhetoric of Renaissance Poetry from Wyatt to Milton* (Berkeley, 1974), pp. 58-72.

10. The names adopted by sonneteers in England or on the continent are not fictive ones intended to conceal; rather they are well-known academic designations or symbolic coinages designed to reveal the identity of the poet and lady to an initiated group. As often as not the poet straightforwardly employs his own name, as did Ronsard in his famous sonnet to Hélène de Surgères, with its line 'Ronsard me celebroit, du temps que j'estois belle' (*Hél.* II, 43:4).

11. George Gascoigne, *A Hundreth sundrie Flowres bounde up in one small Poesie* (London, 1573). Shorter poems in this edition have the running title 'The Devises of Sundry Gentlemen.' Referred to in my text as GI. *The Posies of George Gascoigne Esquire. Corrected, perfected, and augmented by the Authour.* (London, 1575). Shorter poems are divided into three groups, 'Flowers,' 'Hearbes,' and 'Weedes,' and the groups are dispersed among other works in the volume. Referred to as GII.

12. Gabriel Harvey, *Marginalia*, ed. G.C. Moore Smith (Stratford-upon-Avon, 1913), p. 228.

13. Petrarch's famous note on Laura's death, 'Laura propriis virtutibus . . . ' written in his copy of Virgil, is the essential gloss on this problem, and is fully supported by references in his letters, of which the most relevant is *Familiares* II, 9, to Giacomo Colonna. There, in maintaining

Laura was a real person, Petrarch dryly makes clear that an unmediated first person stance is morally central to his poems: 'This wound will heal in time and that Ciceronian saying will apply to me: "Time wounds and time heals," and against this fictitious Laura as you call it, that other fiction of mine, Augustine, will be of help' (Francesco Petrarca, *Rerum familiarum libri*, I - VII, translated Aldo S. Bernardo, (Albany, 1975), p. 102.

14. Paul Zumthor, 'Autobiography in the Middle Ages?' *Genre*, 6 (1973), pp. 29-48.

15. *Certain Sonnets* is attached to the *Old Arcadia* in manuscript Cl and Bo, and the revised *Arcadia* in the 1598 folio. Lyric collections were linked to other works surprisingly often in England; for example, Gascoigne's 1573 *Devises* (GI, see text and note 11) and the much better known instance of Spenser's *Amoretti and Epithalamion*. For some speculations on this see Katherine Duncan-Jones, 'Was the 1609 Shake-speares Sonnets Really Unauthorized?' *RES*, n.s. 34 (1983), pp. 151-71.

16. Sir Philip Sidney, *Astrophil and Stella*, ed. Vanna Gentili (Bari, 1965), p. 104.

17. On the loose organization of *Certain Sonnets* see Ringler, *Poems*, p. 423, p. 425; and Robert Kimbrough, *Sir Philip Sidney* (New York, 1971), p. 102; two attempts to explain it are: Neil Rudenstine, *Sidney's Poetic Development* (Cambridge, Mass., 1967), pp. 277-83, and A.C. Hamilton, *Sir Philip Sidney* (Cambridge, 1977), p. 75.

18. Germaine Warkentin, 'Sidney's Certain Sonnets: Speculations on the Evolution of the Text,' *The Library*, 6th series II (1980), pp. 430-44.

19. James Cotter, 'The Songs in *Astrophil and Stella*,' *SP* 67 (1970), pp. 178-200; Alastair Fowler, *Triumphal Forms* (Cambridge, 1970), pp. 174-80; Thomas P. Roche, Jr., '*Astrophil and Stella*: A Radical Reading,' *Spenser Studies* III (1982), pp. 139-91.

20. The textual problem was finally dealt with by Karl A. Murphy, 'The 109th and 110th Sonnets of *Astrophil and Stella*,' *PQ* 34 (1955), pp. 349-52. See, however, David Kalstone, *Sidney's Poetry: Contexts and Interpretations* (Cambridge, 1965), p. 178.

DIVIDED AIMS IN THE *REVISED ARCADIA*

Maurice Evans

The *Revised Arcadia* is the most capacious of Sidney's literary works, and the one which expresses the widest range of his needs and interests. This paper explores some of the problems to which his peculiar eclecticism gave rise. It is a commonplace that the Renaissance ideal of man involved versatility and excellence in many different fields, but in the case of Sidney, the diversity is extreme. He was an idealist with more than a dash of romantic heroism in his nature, as his behaviour at Zutphen reveals, yet at the same time he had a ruthless and not always compassionate perception of human weakness. He loved heroism but did not believe in heroes. He was charmed by the glamour of old-time chivalry and yet was an earnest student of *realpolitik*: he was interested in people as they are, but he wanted to make them different. His imagination kindled at the old tale of Percy, yet his own theory of poetry was uncompromisingly didactic. He wanted to write: he wanted to do: and it is particularly in Poesy, in the *Revised Arcadia*, that all these incompatibles come most nearly into direct collision.

If we can trust the impression of his language, which becomes incandescent whenever he refers to it, Sidney's deepest pleasure in poetry came from the release of the imagination which it offered . . . 'With a tale forsooth he cometh to you, with a tale which holds children from play, and old men from the chimneycorner. . . ' (*Defence*, 92.9-11) or the familiar description of the Golden World which only the poet can deliver, with its 'forms such as never were in nature, as the Heroes, Demigods, Cyclops, Chimeras, Furies, and such like' (*Defence*, 78.26-27). There is no trace of the moral or didactic here, only an intense delight in the liberation of the imagination from the constraints of the real world which, by his definition, only poetry can give. The emphasis throughout the *Defence* is always upon the 'delight' which poetry arouses, and the fiction which is the source of its power to move us. And yet most readers would agree, I think, that Sidney's greatest writing is mimetic, and that his lasting appeal stems primarily from his ability to describe accurately and unsentimentally a whole range of human weaknesses. The imaginative release into the pastoral world of the *Old Arcadia* leaves less of an impression than the ironic perception of human folly which Sidney gives us; and there can be no doubt that *Astrophil and Stella* is one of the fullest and subtlest studies of conscious self-deception in the language.

In the *Old Arcadia* he kept the two strains separate by exhibiting his main characters in situations where they showed themselves as men rather than as heroes, and channelling most of the idyllicism into the songs and pastoral eclogues; but the *Revised Arcadia* is a different matter. In the 1580s, the disappointment of his ambition to become a great and influential figure in public affairs seems to have driven Sidney to turn to literature as a kind of surrogate action. The *Defence* holds it up as the most powerful form of moral and political rhetoric, of all activities the one most profitable and necessary to the state and the individual. Poetry is to be valued as a practical force, the means of harnessing the imaginative delights of fiction to the direct improvement of society. It is that 'delightful teaching,' he says, 'which must be the right describing note to know a poet by' (*Defence*, 81.37-82.1) and the bland phrase 'delightful teaching,' which insists on a stronger fusion of profit and delight than its original in Horace, is the meeting place for the complex oppositions between the imaginative and the practical, the mimetic and the didactic which exist in Sidney's own nature.

The *Revised Arcadia* is Sidney's attempt to put his theory of poetry into practise. It is more explicitly didactic than anything he had written before; its heroes are more simply heroic, and the third book, which contains most of the wholly new material, seems to be constructed as a demonstration of the virtues appropriate to the old topos of 'Doing and Suffering.' His theory of fiction, and the delightful escape it offers from the foolish world of reality into the golden world of the poet's imagination, does not, on the surface at least, seem to provide much of the basis for a programme of practical moral reform. The argument of the *Defence*, however, derives in part from the tradition of euhemerism, still very much alive in Sidney's day, which offered him a conception of Heroic poetry most congenial to his desires. Euhemerism is, of course, the time-honoured theory concerning the nature of myth, in terms of which the gods of pagan mythology were interpreted as historical figures--heroes, rulers, conquerors, civilizers--who, for their services to mankind, were first revered and then eventually set up as gods or demigods for posterity to worship. The chief agent in this process of elevation was the Heroic poet, and such poets, therefore, are mythmakers who establish the

Divided Aims in the Revised Arcadia

moral myths which guide mankind, and who celebrate through the actions and conquests of their mythical heroes the virtues and vices to be emulated or avoided. For this reason, the poets were, in Puttenham's words, 'the first priests, the first prophets, the first legislators and politicians in the world.'[1] All of these were rôles which held a strong attraction for Sidney. Moreover the tradition was a main source of the moral interpretation of classic epic and heroic romance, and also, of the moral allegory attached to Greek myth which provided the matter for so much Renaissance iconography. This appealed to Sidney's humanism and at the same time offered a moral outlet for the imagination. In this world of moral mythology, didacticism and unlicensed imagination go hand in hand: the chimeras, furies and heroes which so delighted Sidney carried moral meanings as a matter of course. The poet as mythmaker can have it both ways.

The euhemeristic tradition provided Sidney with a variety of myths and mythical settings for his purposes in the *Revised Arcadia*, the most obvious of which is the myth of the Golden Age, which forms the basis of the pastoral vision. The *New Arcadia* abandons the brisk narrative opening of the *Old* and instead establishes the action more firmly within the pastoral, with the idealized shepherds, Strephon and Claius. The pastoral mode, with its long tradition of moral significance derived from its association with the Golden Age and from the Christian overtones of unfallen Eden acquired later, offered Sidney an ideal moral landscape which fused very easily with his vision of the golden world created by the poet's imagination:

> There were hills which garnished their proud heights with stately trees; humble valleys whose base estate seemed comforted with refreshing of silver rivers; meadows enamelled with all sorts of eye-pleasing flowers; thickets, which, being lined with most pleasant shade, were witnessed so to by the cheerful deposition of many well-tuned birds; each pasture stored with sheep feeding with sober security, while pretty lambs with bleating oratory craved the dams' comfort; here a shepherd's boy piping as though he should never be old; there a young shepherdess knitting and withal singing, and it seemed that her voice comforted her hands to work and her hands kept time to her voice's music.[2]

This is very similar to Sidney's account in the *Defence* of the rich tapestry in which the poet can set forth the earth, but it carries also a strong symbolism of ideal order and unfallen innocence; and it can be used, as the Renaissance habitually used it, as a norm against which less ideal scenes can be judged and satirised. Sidney expands his moral field in this way by reminding us that Urania has left Arcadia, and by moving on at once to the description of the shipwreck and the account of the false pastoral idyll of Basilius' country court. This transition into a less than idyllic world enables him to draw on a different range of myths, namely those of the Herculean-type hero whose task is to conquer the ills of a fallen world and restore, if not the Golden, at least the Silver Age. In terms of this he has literary and moral sanction for the creation of heroes of the type of Cyrus, Aeneas or Ulysses in whom is 'each thing to be followed,' and their opposites such as Tantalus or Atreus, in whom there is 'nothing that is not to be shunned.' He already had promising heroes to draw on from the *Old Arcadia* who only needed a little moral stiffening and a wider canvas to fulfill their Herculean roles. Within the framework of Romance, Sidney was able to combine the pastoral and the heroic modes, and use them to provide the appropriate myths for the moral vision and the will to make it prevail. They furnish the constituents of this formula, 'delightful teaching.'

The theory of poetry argued in the *Defence* worked out very well within its limits, but for Sidney it eventually turned into something of a strait jacket. It released his imaginative and didactic impulses and allowed them to yoke together, but it largely denied those mimetic abilities of his genius which found their fullest expression in *Astrophil and Stella*, and which had little place within the conventions and myths of the pastoral or the heroic world. Even the ironic presentation of Musidorus and Pyrocles in love is literary and stereotyped in comparison with the verisimilitude of Astrophil. Nor had Sidney the bridge of allegory which Spenser was able to construct between the real world and that of the Romance which was his medium. The logic of moral myth leads towards allegory, but Sidney's gift was not in that direction: his medium for moral persuasion was necessarily a literal one, the example; and he consistently turns what are potentially allegorical figures into individual people. Anaxius, for instance, is basically the traditional figure of Disdain, but Sidney makes a real person of him. Moreover the world which he describes draws increasingly nearer to the society of his own time, in spite of its classic and pastoral dress. Fiction, as he actually practised it in the *Arcadia* is not the free flight of the imagination, as it is defined in the *Defence*, but something closer to our own understanding of the term in relation, say, to the nineteenth century novel: it is mimetic and related to life, with rules and demands of its own. Yet he was saddled with a didactic theory which demanded the creation of characters in black and white, whose prime function was to demonstrate all the virtues and vices, the graces, skills and corruptions to which the reader must be exposed for his own good. By Book III Sidney may have discovered the difference between reading into the

Divided Aims in the Revised Arcadia

Aeneid whatever moral meanings one may wish to find there and actually composing a poem designed to express those moral meanings. In such a situation, mimesis and rhetoric contradict each other: the characters labour under their moral loads or are fragmented by having to demonstrate forms of excellence which are incompatible with each other. It is difficult to reconcile the Pyrocles in the rôle of practical politician or effective orator with the Pyrocles whose heroic courage can win a battle single-handed; and the Amphialus who knows how to provision an army or allocate responsibility according to the nature of his officers or exploit the different motives of his possible supporters is not the Amphialus who jousts with all comers on his island. Convention and reality, example and fact have become confused: the qualities being exemplified belong to different genres, even to different civilizations. This creates no problem in *The Faerie Queene*, where everything is kept at an equal distance from reality; but it matters greatly in the *New Arcadia*, even though Sidney does his best to minimize the collisions between incompatible elements of his story by the use of an elaborate rhetoric which engrosses the attention in each particular instance and tends to isolate one sequence from another. But this itself fights against the coherence of the structure and the momentum of the action which Sidney is also attempting to achieve.

Sidney's handling of his heroes in particular shows the problems he had created for himself. He believed in the value of the heroic ideal, but he was too much of a realist to believe in heroes as a fact, and he places them firmly within the confines of fiction. Creating them must have been a similar task to that of Milton in creating an Adam before the Fall. Inevitably he turns to heroic literature for his models, and shows great resourcefulness in inventing situations where his characters can demonstrate their qualities; but by the end of Book II, the adventures are becoming stereotyped as they move from the conquest of kings to that of giants and eventually monsters; and by the end of Book III, when most other aspects of human prowess have been exhausted, he is driven for the sake of variety to the verge of 'camp' in the long unfinished fight between Anaxius and Pyrocles in woman's dress. Perhaps the very flippancy of what he found himself doing was a reason why he stopped. Amphialus, indeed, is Sidney's inevitable rebellion against his own technique of moral exemplification: he is the flawed hero, neither an Aeneas nor an Atreus, and the power and realism of his character bursts through the fabric of convention with an almost tragic intensity. He is the clearest evidence that Sidney was not content with the framework which he had chosen and was, in fact, torn between two different modes of moral teaching, the mythical and the dramatic. His treatment of heroines is more successful, partly, perhaps, because he believed that heroism is compatible with a greater degree of human weakness in a woman than he would allow in a man; partly because he had a stronger tradition of female idealism to build on. He succeeds best of all, however, with villains because, presumably, they come closer to real life than heroes--though even here it is not always easy to tell whether he is drawing on life or on the books of characters. Certainly he seems more at home with vice than with virtue; and the fine distinctions which he establishes between vices and follies, and the enormous gallery of pictures, from the boorishness of Dametas to the total egotism of Cecropia, rival even those of Ben Jonson. Here, mimesis and moral example unite in the common truth of the Fall.

Behind this confusion of literary intentions there is, as one would expect, a confusion of philosophies of which Sidney himself, together with many other Renaissance writers, may not have been aware: it is between the fashionable Platonism of the sixteenth century and the interpretations by the Renaissance commentators of the newly discovered *Poetics* of Aristotle. In an earlier paper, Professor Heninger has drawn attention to Sidney's interest in the new empiricism and his sympathy with the mimetic theory of art; and this is obviously true though not, I think, the whole story. Sidney seems to me on many occasions to be trying to follow both Plato and Aristotle at once, without fully recognizing the difference--like a man standing astride Plato's two horses which pull in different directions to use a simile which he himself would have understood very well. The theory of poetry in the *Defence* is a Platonic one, based on the assumption that the divine spark within the human soul, even after the Fall, will kindle to the impression of divinity outside itself. The inspired poet with his erected wit can perceive the divine ideas and embody them in images of ideal truth whose purity can strike, pierce and possess the sight of the soul, so that we are moved to love it whether we will or not. This is deceptively close to the moralised interpretations of Aristotle by the commentators, and the didacticism they attributed to the *Poetics*, reading into it elements of both Plato and Horace. The essential difference, however, lies in the fact that Platonism, as Sidney interpreted it, exerts its didactic pressure at the unconscious level: we are moved by the truths of poetry without knowing why, and often against our will; and it is only after we have been moved that the speaking picture defines for us the reason, so that men may 'know that goodness whereunto they are moved.' Catharsis, on the other hand, is normally understood by the Renaissance critics as a conscious and rational process: we seek to emulate those characters we admire and prudently flee the courses which end in tragedy. Sidney does not seem to distinguish between the two didactic modes, and draws on both traditions indiscriminately. There can be no doubt, however, that he fully understood the implications of Aristotle's Mimesis in relation to plot, character, and structure. In its close control of supporting detail and its stricter definition of motive, the *New Arcadia* shows the unmistakable influence of what Aristotle had said about probability and necessity: the plot proceeds from the nature of the characters and in turn defines them; and the main action moves forward with its own inevitable inner logic. Mimesis in this sense does not mix happily with any brand of overt didacticism.

The consequences of Sidney's divided aims can be seen in his very uncertain control of the 'speaking pictures' which form the basis of his 'delightful teaching.' They are explicitly didactic in intention, and their very name suggests a static tableau which is hostile to the verisimilitude of a dramatic story; yet, as Professor Heninger has suggested, the emphasis on the visual derives from Aristotle's Mimesis and is reinforced by Horace's tag 'ut pictura poesis,' in consequence of which the association of poetry and painting dominated poetic theory for the next two hundred years. Sidney himself in the *Defence* relates his 'speaking pictures' to mimesis and endows them with the Horatian function, to teach and delight, although, as we have seen, their method of teaching is basically Platonic; and with a pedigree as mixed as this some confusion is inevitable. At times he takes material which is mimetic and dramatic by nature and tries to make it perform the functions of emblem or hieroglyph; or alternatively, he attempts to fit pictures which are frankly emblematic into a mimetic context. He is most successful when he keeps the two strains separate from each other and uses his pictures as emblems. The brilliant picture embodying the nature of democracy, as Sidney understood it (p. 383), is a good example; or the little vignette describing Pamela at Prayer:

> But this prayer sent to heaven from so heavenly a creature, with such a fervent grace as if devotion had borrowed her body to make of itself a most beautiful representation; with her eyes so lifted to the skyward that one would have thought they had begun to fly thitherward to take their place among their fellow stars; her naked hands raising up their whole length and, as it were, kissing one another, as if the right had been the picture of Zeal, and the left of Humbleness, which both united themselves to make their suits more acceptable: lastly, all her senses being rather tokens than instruments of her inward motions.
> (p. 464)

This is explicitly a picture and an emblem: her appearance has been made a 'token' of what is to be expressed. Sidney has taken Pamela out of her narrative context and turned her

Divided Aims in the Revised Arcadia

into an illustration for a book of devotions. He is, of course, drawing on the familiar tradition of memory images: the picture of Pamela with her hands raised in the traditional posture of prayer stays in the memory, and will serve as a perpetual reminder that the constituents of true prayer are zeal and humility.

Sidney is less certain in his control, however, when he uses speaking pictures to arouse our feelings at moments of high drama, such as the scourging of Philoclea, for example (pp. 551-2), or the tragic death of Parthenia:

> . . . her roundy sweetly swelling lips a little trembling, as though they kissed their neighbour death; in her cheeks the whiteness striving by little and little to get upon the rosiness of them; her neck, a neck indeed of alabaster, displaying the wound, which with most dainty blood laboured to drown his own beauties, so here was a river of purest red, there an island of perfectest white, each giving lustre to the other . . .
>
> (p. 528)

The moment is one of great tragedy but it does not come over in this way. The dying Parthenia is lost under the facade of ornament; the pain is distanced, and instead of pity and fear we have the sort of pleasing pathos to be found in a play such as Ford's *The Broken Heart*. This is a typical example of how Sidney handles tragic situation, and it is not easy to be sure of his intention. He may have been striving for a genuinely tragic effect but have failed to realize that speaking pictures are better at defining for the mind than embodying for the feelings: he may not have recognized that poetry is not in fact speaking picture, that words do not work like dramatic images, and that verbal descriptions produce different effects from real pictures. He may even have misunderstood Aristotle's conception of the tragic pleasure, which he himself calls 'delightful terribleness.' He agrees with Aristotle that Mimesis by its very nature gives pleasure, no matter what is being imitated; but in practice he seems never quite to trust this, and tends to embellish his tragic moments with a display of fine and witty rhetoric to ensure that the reader is adequately pleased. His descriptions of battles, for example, anticipate those of Nashe, in the way they wrap up the ugly facts in conceited language and humour which at times borders on hilarity, as in the very funny account of Pyrocles' slaughter of the rebels.

There are signs, however, that Sidney was aware of the problems of communication and was constantly exploring and developing his techniques. If I may consider a final example, the great account in Book III of the first battle between Amphialus and the forces of Philanax shows Sidney attempting to separate the pictorial from the speaking dimensions of his speaking picture, the mimetic from the emblematic. The sequence begins with the simple, unaffected, purely mimetic account of the death of the young Agenor '. . . of all that army the most beautiful . . . full of jollity in conversation and lately grown a lover,' who puts his lance in rest 'as careful of comely carrying it as if the mark had been but a ring and the lookers on ladies.' It is a deeply moving passage which could almost come out of the *Iliad*. In the battle which follows, the weapons themselves seem to take over the field . . . 'Some lances, according to the metal they met, . . . did stain themselves in blood . . . But their office was quickly inherited, either by (the prince of weapons) the sword, or by some heavy mace or biting axe which, hunting still the weakest chase, sought ever to light there where smallest resistance might worse prevent mischief.' This is bordering on allegory, but the contrast it makes between the inhuman, impersonal quality of the weapons and the frailty and vulnerability of the human beings turns the pity of the first sequence into fear, and lifts the whole passage to the level of genuine tragedy. Having first moved us, Sidney goes on to show us why we are moved in the final sequence which defines in a great set-piece the unnaturalness of war. This is the famous battle symphony, in which the clashing of armour and the groans of the dying provide the orchestration for 'that ill-agreeing music,' and the logic of all normal relations is put into reverse: the horses lay upon their lords instead of carrying them; the earth instead of burying men is buried by them, and the legs, having been cut off from their bodies, 'being discharged of their heavy burden, were grown heavier' (pp. 468-9). There is a complete change of key here from an emotional to an intellectual level, which could have led from one kind of tragedy to another, from one of character to one of ideas. In fact this does not happen; as is so often the case, Sidney is trying too hard: the extended and witty paradoxes, the puns on dispossessed and disinherited, the half jokes about the legs and fingers are ultimately too flippant for the moral point he is making; and what comes through is an impression of the brilliance and virtuosity of Sidney's own technique, as if he cared more for his picture than for what it was saying.

It is possible that this was the effect which Sidney intended, and that his elaborate rhetoric throughout the *Arcadia* is a deliberate means of distancing the often horrific actions from the reader, so as not to fright the ladies who read it. Certainly this is the overall effect of the work: *The Arcadia*, to our profit and pleasure is a Romance, not an earnest moral treatise. Whether he would or could have redressed the moral balance if he had finished it, we cannot tell; but there is no point in speculating on this, any more than on Sir Thomas Browne's questions about what song the syrens sang, or what name Achilles assumed when he hid himself among women--though to the latter question Sidney might well have had an answer. The name would, of course, have been Zelmane.

NOTES

1. George Puttenham, *The Art of English Poesie*, in G. Gregory Smith (ed.), *Elizabethan Critical Essays* (London, 1904), II, p. 6.
2. Maurice Evans (ed. and introduction), *The Countess of Pembroke's Arcadia* (Harmondsworth, 1977), pp. 69-70. Quotations from the *Arcadia* in the present essay are taken from this edition and incorporated into the text.

ASTROPHIL'S STELLA AND STELLA'S ASTROPHIL

Robert L. Montgomery

In 1972, Richard Lanham argued that *Astrophil and Stella* has no 'aristic' structure, that it is not centered in self-analysis, that it is 'outward' and non-meditative, and, most surprisingly, that it is autobiographical in a very direct and obvious way. All the shifts in mood, the ironies, the various postures and protestations must be referred to one exclusive motive--Sidney's thinly and transparently veiled effort to seduce Penelope Rich. The sequence is thus not a finished work of art, but instead the raw data of a none-too-creditable episode in Sidney's youth. All the poems are simply, in a phrase Lanham borrows from Kenneth Burke, maneuvers in Sidney's 'impure persuasion.'[1]
    Anyone familiar with Sidney's career and with the scholarship on the text of the sequence--especially Ringler's conclusions about the composition of the songs (*Poems*, pp. xlv-xlvi, 484)--will at once notice the weaknesses in this view. Lanham's effort to explain all the poems by making Stella the only audience is much too simple--an exercise in reduction that solves problems by pretending they don't exist. Most of us would concede that Sidney's own experience is in some sense the basis for the sequence, and so Sidney and Astrophil have a measure of identity. But the invented persona allows the poet a crucial detachment, and it permits also a kind of indeterminacy, giving the sequence a subtle interplay not only between biography and fiction, but also between Astrophil as a single, coherent fictional character and the consciously shaped and articulated selves deliberately fashioned and offered to the attention of Stella. But if Lanham oversimplifies an important element in the sequence, he raises an issue we should be interested in--and that is the question of the *ethos* Astrophil adopts for himself and the manner in which he characterizes Stella. These two characterizations and the ways in which they are sorted out are my concerns here.
    In the early sonnets Astrophil offers a codified and idealized Stella: she is love and beauty, 'so true a Deitie'

shrined in flesh, 'most faire, most cold,' a figure of 'miraculous power,' a 'heavenly guest,' a source of poetic inspiration. These and other epithets compose a poet's figure in that her beauty is the beauty of a work of art and her virtue, if we allow for Petrarchan hyperbole, is equally fixed and iconographic. Midway through the sequence Stella concedes she loves Astrophil, but with 'a love not blind,' so morally she remains nearly unambiguous, a figure of power and control. And this moral posture is one of the sources of her appeal to Astrophil. The other, of course, is her appearance, or as Astrophil at one point says, her 'outside,' and in this guise she compels desire.

What I have just summarized is the schematic Stella, the radically simplified figure drawn from convention, outlined in witty blazons and well-established epithets, so familiar that we scarcely any more give her our attention, except sometimes to see her as an awkward, 'artificial' presence. But it seems to me that the blazoned, almost dehumanized, Stella is significant, because it is her unyielding 'virtue' (rather improbable given what we know of the later career of Penelope Rich) that determines the outcome of the sequence and thus brings together the conventional Stella, the person created by Astrophil's enthusiastic celebration and the dramatic Stella, the person who disconcertingly refuses his suit. Astrophil's Stella is therefore first of all a figure of stylized absolutes, and so long as these absolutes are simply qualities that identify and define, they remain a coherent whole consistent with one another. But they are not really objective characterizations, or at least not only that. We must look on them as projections of Astrophil's own vision and wish, and in their capacity to translate love's impact on Astrophil they become opposite and incompatible, a condition anticipated in the turn Sidney gives to Platonic philosophy in Sonnet 25:

> The wisest scholer of the wight most wise
> By *Phoebus'* doome, with sugred sentence sayes,
> That Vertue, if it once met with our eyes,
> Strange flames of *Love* it in our soules would raise.

Astrophil's momentary conflation of virtue and beauty serves to emphasize his and our sense of their different implications. The sonnet concludes:

> Vertue's great beautie in that face I prove,
> And find th'effect, for I do burne in love.

As we know from other poems and from the set of conventions within which the sequence operates, virtue demands service, admiration, and respect for Stella's honor, but excludes the kind of love Astrophil has in mind.

As an emblematic figure, Stella embodies the terms of ethical and emotional conflict that we routinely suppose defines Petrarchism as a system of balanced and unresolved moral tension. The impasse between female refusal and male importunity was ordinarily expressed so as to forbid reconciliation or compromise. Dialectically the demands of virtue 'killed' desire, and the demands of desire implied the destruction of virtue. The resolution for Petrarch, or for Fulke Greville, is to shift the discourse to a transcendent religious vision, to look at the situation retrospectively, from a perspective beyond the claims of desire. Petrarch's Laura after her death occupies a different symbolic status in his consciousness than she did in the poems which include her as a living figure. Greville violently rejects passion as the ground of human depravity and puts in its place a bitter, almost punitive vision of religious judgment. These are essentially non-dramatic resolutions. They provide an ending by altering the terms of discourse and allowing the poet to shift his central intellectual stance.

Sidney's procedure is different. He conducts the sequence so that it ends only with a plea for release from his emotionally exhausted protagonist, using convention to portray Astrophil as the suffering, though often self-consciously witty victim. Stella's eyes set him afire--'Of touch they are, and poor I am their straw'--or as Sonnet 16 concludes,

> In her sight I a lesson new have speld,
>   I now have learn'd Love right, and learn'd even so,
>   As who by being poisond doth poison know.

As Sonnet 5 indicates, Astrophil from the beginning is aware of the moral objections to his inclinations, but Stella's influence seizes and dominates his existence to the point that such objections become the occasion for wit or scorn. Sonnet 23 expresses this condition as well as any other:

> O fooles, or over-wise, alas the race
>   Of all my thoughts hath neither stop nor start,
>   But only *Stella's* eyes and *Stella's* hart.

The possibility of an utterly static situation is implicit here, and if it were allowed to stand unmolested, the sequence might then possess a certain kind of symmetry and completeness. Astrophil would employ his mind and heart entirely in contemplation of Stella, and presumably as poet he would simply devote himself to her description and praise. The matching characterization of Astrophil as victim, as isolated prisoner of love and as worshiper, would be an important part of such a still-life. But any possibility that that might happen is abruptly dismissed in the very next poem, 'Rich fooles there be, whose base and filthy hart.' The contrast between Sonnets 23 and 24, between a declaration of exclusive worship on the one hand and bitter jealousy and scarcely controlled desire on the other could hardly be more abrupt or more pointed. Hence the stylized emblematic elements are never totally destroyed or banished from our sight. They remain in the wings and on occasion re-enter, as a reminder of the underlying terms of conflict on which Astrophil's condition is based. They re-enact from time to time an ideal brought on stage only to be dismissed yet again.[2]

We should also notice that for the time being the abrupt outburst against Lord Rich seems merely to punctuate Astrophil's repeated expressions of passion, devotion, praise, distraction, and bondage: the succession of emotional states argues an inner chaos of which Astrophil is well aware and which is important in conveying to us an impression of authenticity. Sonnet 33 once again brings us back to the hard circumstance of Stella's marriage, a circumstance which has to be set against the drift of those poems that look to an idealized situation. But except for this one event, the discourse of love at this stage of the sequence is almost entirely derived from and directed at the idea of Stella's power, and however Astrophil presents himself, whether deliberately or obliquely through the tone of his utterance, he does so as a form of response to that fact. Just as an example we might glance briefly at Sonnet 35, 'What may words say, or what may words not say,' a poem that ends in witty celebration: 'Not thou by praise, but praise in thee is raisde:/It is a praise to praise, when thou art praisde.' The hyperbole carries the Petrarchan schemes about as far as they can go--to the point that Stella becomes the source of passion, honor, fame, and praise, as well as a power that obliterates any ordinary distinction between language as truth and prevarication.

The exaggeration is of course just that, an effort to express the farthest reach of stylized characterization, but not an effort to imagine it governing the course of events. Rather it stands as an index of imagined and impossible-to-maintain perfection of the kind painted by Marvell in the first few lines of 'To His Coy Mistress.' And if exaggeration measures the poet's and the lover's wit and works against the sense of emotional authenticity, it is also, at least in part, the means by which the static Petrarchan situation is ruptured.

Sonnets 44 and 45 suggest just such dual functions: in 44 he supposes that he gets no pity because her mind in the fashion of an artist can change the sobs of his annoys to 'tunes of joyes.' But in 45, wittily invoking the Aristotelian concept of catharsis, Astrophil begs Stella to turn him into a tale so she can pity him: 'I am not I, pity the tale of me.' His sophistry now wants to use the resources of fictionalizing for persuasion, but part of the wit is of course the open, bare-faced effrontery of the double senses of 'pity' and 'tale.' Yet as conventional lover Astrophil claims that both his passion and his suffering are genuine: they have to be to match the image of Stella as all-powerful.

And Sonnet 45 begins by asserting 'Stella oft sees the *very* face of wo.' Surely the poem demands that its first and last lines stand in contrast--the true face of woe set against the saucy notion that Stella should pretend he is a work of fiction in order to submit to him.

So for Astrophil the alternative to the fixed ethos of the Petrarchan servant is the volatile and aggressive role of the witty seducer. This role is introduced and maintained by a series of reversals, an element in the structure of a number of the poems in the middle of the sequence. The procedure is familiar from Sonnet 5, where the last line flatly contradicts the sense and tone of the previous thirteen, poising the irreducible fact of love against the Platonic and Christian argument that beauty is illusory and that Cupid is a deity fashioned by human wish and foolishness.

The sonnets of the middle section of the sequence set in this mold are 52, 63, 68, 71, 72, 76, and 77. The last two, 76 and 77, exemplify the type most obviously. Each develops a line of thought and a kind of ample epideictic style through thirteen lines almost to the point of parody, though not quite that far. Each celebrates Stella's power and Stella herself as a work of art. Together they pretty completely sum up the Petrarchan testament, both invoking the imagery of the sun and the eyes. Here are their initial quatrains:

> She comes, and streight therewith her shining
>   twins do move
>   Their rayes to me, who in her tedious absence lay
>   Benighted in cold wo, but now appeares my day,
> The onely light of joy, the onely warmth of *Love.*
>
>   (Sonnet 76)

and

> Those lookes, whose beames be joy, whose motion is
>   delight,
> That face, whose lecture shewes what perfect beautie is:
> That presence, which doth give darke hearts a living
>   light:
> That grace, which *Venus* weeps that she her selfe doth
>   misse.
>
>   (Sonnet 77)

These are lines of great beauty; they are also the utterance of the subservient, patient, and obedient Astrophil, or they are if we leave them and their succeeding lines to themselves. But of course they are cancelled, or perhaps not so much cancelled as rocked out of balance by the fourteenth lines. Sonnet 76 turns the sun image--which Sidney uses often from the first sonnet on to refer to Stella's god-like power--in a different direction. The wit is almost like Donne's. Here is the final tercet:

Asrtophil's Stella and Stella's Astrophil

> No wind, no shade can coole, what helpe then in my case,
> But with short breath, long lookes, staid feet and
>   walking hed,
> Pray that my sunne go down with meeker beames to bed.

In these poems we have two voices, two Astrophils, one uttering everything called for by his character as suffering worshiper, the other seeking to bridge the gulf between adoration and desire by an elaborate pun. (We might add that there is implied in the rhetoric of desire another less remote and immovable Stella, but her only concession is to return Astrophil's love without in the least entertaining his lust.) Rather self-consciously the second Astrophil is quite aware of the first. This is perhaps more evident in Sonnet 77, where he blazons Stella (those looks, that face, that presence, etc.) and then gives the catalogue two conclusions:

> That conversation sweet, where such high comforts be,
> As consterd in true speech, the name of heavn'n it beares,
> Makes me in my best thoughts and quietst judgement see,
> That in no more but these I might be fully blest....

The last line of this quotation is line thirteen, and it mentions a possibility raised more than once in the sequence, but always eventually overriden. Astrophil, as contemplative adorer, as fixed and accepting unrequited lover, is always invoked to be displaced. The point has sometimes been made that the raising of this alternative, the utterances of the Astrophil who is content with a 'virtuous' love indicates the didactic point of the sequence, that it should be understood as demonstrating an Augustinian judgment on sensual appetite, that Astrophil's witty rejections of good counsel and restraint mask an immature neglect to take seriously the moral and spiritual risks he incurs. This argument has some merit,[3] but I think Sidney's purpose is less the urging of a moral lesson than a demonstration by means of various ironies of psychological disarray.

Although the dialectics of convention permit Stella to return Astrophil's love--this much dramatic or narrative development is tolerable because it allows the situation still to remain one in which honor is preserved and a virtuous affection can be maintained--emotionally it is a frozen, static kind of coherence, at least from the point of view of Astrophil. The effort to reconcile passion and virtue simply keeps breaking down. The power of desire is finally greater than Stella's power and Sonnet 77 can't possibly conclude with the line 'That in no more but these I might be fully blest.' And we have line 14:

> Yet ah, my Mayd'n Muse doth blush to tell her best.

Astrophil's wit is largely devoted to this subversive voice, attempting to discredit both the idealized Stella and

the values that define his social and moral obligations. And
his wit has another use: it lets us know that Astrophil is
quite aware of the two opposed worlds--of worship and desire--
and of the terms of their incompatibility.

In another sense Stella is also a subversive figure,
especially the dramatic Stella, the person who actually denies
Astrophil's suit. As he says, she frustrates his complaints
by turning them into tunes of joys. She returns his love
eventually but of course will not allow consummation, insisting that she loves 'a Love not blind.' The fourth song defi-
nitively records the failure of Astrophil's suit, and the
fifth song, though it may well, as Ringler supposes, have been
written before *Astrophil and Stella*,[4] begins by sketching out
the kind of coherence Astrophil enjoys and expects so long as
he thinks there is a chance of persuading his mistress. The
opening stanza is instructive:

> While favour fed my hope, delight with hope was brought,
> Thought waited on delight, and speech did follow thought:
> Then grew my tongue and pen records unto thy glory:
> I thought all words were lost, that were not spent of
> thee;
> I thought each place was darke, but where thy lights
> would be,
> And all eares worse than deafe, that heard not out thy
> storie.

The figure *gradatio* or climax, which Sidney uses so memorably
in Sonnets 1 and 2 to establish a chain of coherent reasoning
that has to be abandoned, is repeated here, recapitulating
some of the themes I have been considering, but this time in
the context of Astrophil's presentation of himself as poet.
The stanzas express Astrophil as praiser of Stella, suggesting that the motive for praise is hope and projecting a clear
and logical connection between the vision of Stella's 'glory,'
devotion to her, and the fashioning of poetry as totally and
exclusively dedicated to her: 'I thought all words were lost,
that were not spent of thee.' Other features of this poem do
indeed seem anomalous, but the theme of a totally exclusive
poetic effort is consistent with all the poems in which
Astrophil discusses the poetic art and his role as a poet.
Indeed throughout the sequence his status as a poet derives
only from his attention to Stella.

Some of Sidney's critics have tended to accept Astrophil's portrait of himself at face value, reading Sonnet 1
and the subsequent poems which discuss issues of invention,
style, subject, inspiration, and the like, as straightforward
and entirely appropriate cautions against derivative, insincere, and sterile modes of writing.[5] It has not been
difficult to find echoes of some of these poems in *An Apology
for Poetry*, thus ensuring Sidney's complicity in the critical
utterances of his protagonist. One result is to break those

Astrophil's Stella and Stella's Astrophil

poems out of the dramatic frame of the sequence and treat them as if they were Sidney's effort to tell us what kind of poetry he is writing. Not the least of the problems thus raised is the fact that Astrophil, on the evidence of the styles in the sequence itself, violates the principles of composition he so aggressively proclaims. Hallett Smith some time ago argued that a way around this difficulty is to suppose that Astrophil is talking about imaginary, fictional poems which we, as readers of the sequence, never see.[6] We can, I think, go one step further: we can agree with Smith that *Astrophil and Stella* should be read as a work of fiction, but we need not worry about whether certain poems refer to other unavailable poems which we never see. Perhaps this was Sidney's intention, or perhaps not. What seems to me crucial is that we regard Astrophil's presentation of himself as poet as an extension of his ethos as lover.

As poet Astrophil is as jaunty one moment and sorrowful the next as he is in his role of lover. In Sonnet 1 he wryly proclaims his conversion from textbook poet to one who consults his own experience, but in Sonnet 2 something quite different emerges: writing becomes a mode of wish fulfilment that expresses, inadvertently, self-deception and pain. In Sonnet 3 poets who work within convention or fashion, who employ disguise, ornate diction, and strangeness are unflatteringly compared to himself and his much more direct and simple method of "reading" Stella's face and then copying it. Sonnet 6 thrusts Astrophil's self-proclaimed sincerity against the clichés of Petrarchist expression:

I can speake what I feele, and feele as much as they,
But thinke that all the Map of my state I display,
When trembling voice brings forth that I do *Stella* love.

Sonnet 15 recapitulates Astrophil's contempt for fashion, conventional expression, and Petrarchist emotionalism--these "bewray a want of inward tuch'--and once again sets Stella as subject and inspiration firmly against them. The twins of sincerity and directness are yet again insisted on in Sonnet 28, which has the added value of linking these stirring poetic virtues to Astrophil's defiant rejection of the general contempt for lovesickness:

When I say '*Stella*,' I do meane the same
  Princesse of Beautie, for whose only sake
  The raines of *Love* I love, though never slake,
And joy therein, though Nations count it shame.

Most such poems offer us a cocksure Astrophil, repeating the themes of simplicity and sincerity in such a way as to try to persuade Stella, his readers, and himself that poetry thus employed can be at once the authentic expression of

emotion and the effective instrument of female surrender.
What Astrophil does is to offer a kind of simplified view of
the poet as sophist, a view foreshadowed in Sonnet 1 and reiterated periodically through the first two-thirds of the
sequence. Its logic is summed up in Sonnet 74:

> I never drank of *Aganippe* well,
> Nor ever did in shade of *Tempe* sit;
> And Muses scorne with vulgar braines to dwell:
> Poor Layman I, for sacred rites unfit.
>   Some do I heare of Poets' furie tell,
> But (God wot) wot not what they meane by it:
> And this I sweare by blackest brooke of hell,
> I am no pick-purse of another's wit.
>   How falles it then, that with so smooth an ease
> My thoughts I speake, and what I speake doth flow
> In verse, and that my verse best wits doth please?
> Guesse we the cause: 'What, is it thus?' Fie, no:
>   'Or so?' Much lesse. 'How then?' Sure thus it is:
> My lips are sweet, inspired with *Stella's* kisse.

The assertions here differ from earlier ones only in the new
circumstance of the kiss Stella has granted. Otherwise, we
have the same confident poet trumpeting his individuality and
attributing the successful coherence of his verse to Stella.
  The view of poetry and the poet thus offered is clearly
meant by Astrophil as a form of self-justification, as its
tone suggests, but it is sharply at odds with another mood,
initially expressed in Sonnet 2 and also reiterated from time
to time as in Sonnet 34, where wit and writing are acknowledged to have consequences quite disconcertingly different
from those intended. This mood, in which poetic composition
offers neither relief from suffering nor persuasive results,
is not one which Astrophil is willing to maintain. It is only
a momentary fissure in the fabric of confident poetic self-
assertion: as the next poem, Sonnet 35, shows us, Astrophil
evades despair by wit--'Wit learnes in thee perfection to
expresse'--but in so doing he also slides off the whole question of whether his posture as sincere, suffering, praising
poet is a true statement of the case. That question emerges
in Sonnet 55, where Astrophil notes that he has indeed called
on the Muses and employed a florid style, though in vain.
From now on, he concludes, he will simply call on Stella's
name.
  This poem reminds us, if we have not already discovered
the point, that Astrophil's various styles and repeated claims
of poetic simplicity and authenticity are really at bottom
strategies of desire. Read in the light of the motive of
seduction, Astrophil's self-characterization as poet has to be
narrowly construed. However interesting the critical sonnets
are, however much they may please us as favoring an art rooted

in experience rather than convention, or as efforts to establish a mode of writing that balances convention with freshness, their main significance is to be found in the rhetorical situation. They express the ethos of the hopeful but frustrated lover, not Sidney's own critical stance or the general rightness of a kind of style.

It is also possible to argue that even if Astrophil's professions of authentic feeling and inspiration could not be read as self-serving, as designed to influence Stella towards the bedroom, they would still be suspect. It would be incorrect to propose that Sidney or his contemporaries would argue for a deliberately derivative or insincere poetic, but Astrophil's sneers at ornate, indirect, allegorical, or conventional verse belittle modes of writing that were perfectly acceptable in the sixteenth century and were practised by poets as considerable as Ronsard and Spenser and, indeed, Sidney himself. In order to accept Astrophil's critical views as Sidney's own, we would have to ignore Sidney's rhetorical skill, the range and variety and subtlety of his use of the speaking voice, his management of a score of poetic conventions, and above all we would have to retreat to the identification of Astrophil and Sidney which so severely constricts the interest of the work.

The narrowness of Astrophil's ethos and its real limitations from Sidney's point of view have already been touched on: when the role of downright, simple worshipping and suffering poet fails, then, as the protagonist acknowledges, words also fail or if the poet turns inward, his poetic offers insufficient resources for a genuine self-examination. As Sonnet 94 tells us, grief has so clouded his mind that 'inbent eyes/Can scarce discerne the shape of mine own paine.' And if we return now to Sonnet 2, which must be regarded as introductory to the entire sequence, we can find Sidney's indirect hand demonstrating the paradoxical results of a poetic whose coherence and value are dissolved in the lover's self-delusion:[7]

> Now even that footstep of lost libertie
> Is gone, and now like slave-borne *Muscovite*
> I call it praise to suffer Tyrannie;
> And now employ the remnant of my wit,
>   To make my self beleve, that all is well,
>   While with a feeling skill I paint my hell.

The confession is important. Astrophil has employed wit not only to argue that his pursuit of Stella is defensible, 'that all is well,' but also to argue dishonestly that there is no inconsistency between the ideal of virtue and the claims of desire. The fundamental irony of the sequence, which is evident in so many of its elements, is nowhere more pointed than here in the unintended consequences of the rhetoric of

Astrophil's Stella and Stella's Astrophil

persuasion.

NOTES

1. Richard A. Lanham, '*Astrophil and Stella*: Pure and Impure Persuasion,' *ELR*(1972), pp. 100-15.

2. On the point that Petrarch and Sidney keep recapitulating the terms and contexts of passion, see Germaine Warkentin's interesting article, 'Sidney and the Supple Muse: Compositional Procedures in Some Sonnets of *Astrophil and Stella*,' *Studies in the Literary Imagination* 15(1982), pp.37-48. Warkentin argues (p. 48) that for Petrarch each poem is 'a new beginning' in the attempt to reconstruct the shattered and divided self and that Sidney's grasp of the rhetorical principles used by Petrarch to shape this effort justifies the title of 'English Petrarke.'

3. See, for example, Andrew D. Weiner, 'Structure and "Fore Conceit" in *Astrophil and Stella*,' *TSLL*(1974), pp. 1-25. Weiner views the work as elaborately didactic, organized in five stages, giving Astrophil five 'identities' in succession. The sequence, 'under the guise of telling a feigned story, is a series of discreet attacks by the poet upon the imagination [and, hence, the will] of the reader' (p. 22).

4. For a different way of understanding Astrophil's presentation of himself as poet, see Jacqueline T. Miller, '"Love Doth Hold My Hand,": Writing and Wooing in the Sonnets of Sidney and Spenser,' *ELH* 46(1979), pp. 541-58. She proposes that Sidney's own creative imagination and control are in conflict with his strategic claim that these powers are all surrendered to Stella and to love. This view is weakened by her assumption that the critical sonnets are all Sidney's utterances, not Astrophil's. Moreover, one would think that if there were such a tension, Sidney would exploit it more openly, as he does other points of conflict in the sequence. Still another reading is that of Richard B. Young, 'English Petrarke: A Study of Sidney's *Astrophel and Stella*,' *Three Studies in the Renaissance: Sidney, Jonson, Milton* (Yale, 1958), p. 9: 'Sidney has exploited the technical problem, the relation of manner and matter, as the chief means of presenting the dramatic problem, the relation of lady and lover.' Young's reading is closer to my own, but he considers Astrophil's accounts of himself as poet as ultimately sincere, where I propose to view them as maneuvers only.

5. Cf. J.W. Lever, *The Elizabethan Love Sonnet* (London, 1956), p. 53. Neil Rudenstine, *Sidney's Poetic Development* (Cambridge, Mass., 1967) notes (pp. 197-98) that the critical sonnets can be read as strategic in Astrophil's pursuit of Stella, but he also says that 'Astrophel expresses a complex attitude toward style similar to that which Sidney articulated in the *Apologie*....' My own *Symmetry and Sense: The Poetry of Sir Philip Sidney* (Austin, 1961) expressed a similar attitude and examined Astrophil as an honestly self-critical figure.

6. Hallett C. Smith, *Elizabethan Poetry: A Study in Conventions, Meaning, and Expression* (Cambridge, Mass., 1952), p. 145. Smith also remarks (p. 143) of the critical sonnets: 'We can digest from these a doctrine about love poetry, and perhaps by implication about all poetry; more significantly, we can use these ideas, properly understood, as a method of analysis of the cycle itself.'

7. Alan Sinfield's important article, 'Sidney and Astrophil,' *SEL*(1980), pp. 25-41, makes a strong case for not confusing Sidney and his protagonist on the grounds that as readers we are meant to identify with Astrophil and then recognize our own capacity for the errors Sidney makes him reveal in himself.

SIDNEIAN INDIRECTION: THE ETHICAL IRONY OF *ASTROPHIL AND STELLA*

Charles S. Levy

This paper attempts to clarify and to refine the growing sense of the ironic structure of *Astrophil and Stella* that we owe to the work of many students of the poem; I am particularly indebted to a discussion held several years ago at Kalamazoo, Michigan, of a paper in which Thomas Roche analyzes the moral incongruity of some features of Astrophil's behavior in their traditional context of Christian doctrine.[1] Altering contexts, I should like to venture a similar comparison between the second song of Sidney's poem and the third elegy of the Roman poet Propertius's first book, his so-called *Cynthia Monobiblos*. By reference to this celebrated Propertian model and in particular to the climactic emphasis the elegy places upon the voice of the woman and upon her bitter indictment of her lover's faithless behavior, Astrophil's principal offense against his beloved in song 2 is by no means that of stealing a kiss from her while she sleeps. Cynthia's lover clearly had far more than that in mind, a fact that instead may at least momentarily increase our sympathy for Astrophil during the series of further *basia*. Astrophil's principal offense here against Stella lies rather in his failure to give her a speaking role of any kind in this early song, by contrast with songs 4 and 8 to come—a contrast which enforces that with Propertius's poem, the entire last movement of which belongs to Cynthia and to the passionately just complaint her lover thus implicitly acknowledges:

    So you've come at last, and only because that other
                                            woman
      has thrown you out and closed the doors against you.
    Where have you spent the night—this night that belonged
                                                  to me?
      Look at you, creeping back with the dawn, a wreck!
    It'd do you good to have to spend the sort of night
       you make me spend—you'd learn what cruelty is.
    I sat up over my loom, trying to stave off sleep,

>   then tired of that and played the lyre a while.
>   And under my breath I told myself what it's like to be
>   jilted,
>   and thought of the hours you spend in another's bed.
>   Then sleep touched me with soothing wings and brought
>   release;
>   but my last thoughts were thoughts of the grief you
>   bring me.[2]

We need only avail ourselves of the perspective afforded by feminist criticism, for example, in order clearly to recognize the contrast in question. By her enforced silence, Stella in some ways speaks even more insistently than does Cynthia--*tacet, clamat*; by his exclusion of Stella's voice, Astrophil's shame becomes in some ways still deeper than that of the Propertian lover; in short, by the light this contrast throws, we see more clearly illuminated Astrophil's crucial error in love, of which his weakness for the stolen kiss is but a symptom: Astrophil fails systematically to take Stella seriously as a moral and emotional being, and from that failure flows the otherwise avoidable disaster of song 8 and all that follows. The title of Sidney's poem, as Roche pointed out, is on the coordinate model of *Romeo and Juliet*;[3] in no case could we think of the work as being a *Stella Monobiblos*.

Other kinds of perspective may well suggest other foil-texts--or other foil-texts may suggest other perspectives and other insights. For example, Putzel comments on the 'mawkish acquiescence' to which one glance from Stella reduces Astrophil in Sonnet 47, arguably an instance of the failure to establish his personal autonomy that McCoy finds everywhere characteristic of Astrophil.[4] Astrophil does put up an abortive struggle in that sonnet, to be sure: 'I may, I must, I will, I can, I will, I do/Leave following that, which it is gaine to misse./Let her go.' Moreover, in the very rhythm of insistent resolve that we hear in the first of these verses, we may catch an echo now of Catullus, of something of the vehemence pervading his *carmen* 8, 'Miser Catulle, desinas ineptire,' 'Stop fouling up!'. The earlier poet expresses the desperate obstinacy of a too little unwilling lover, voicing that obstinacy like Astrophil in short bursts: 'perfer, obdura,' 'stand it! and don't give in!' (11), and again, 'destinatus obdura' (19).[5] Finally, it must be conceded, Catullus's great vehemence itself suggests that he might in fact give in if he had the occasion. These are but the similarities, however, that render the contrast between the two lyrics striking and that thus indirectly point up Astrophil's ultimate failure of resolve, for the lyrics differ greatly in their ultimate dramatic effect:[6] Catullus does stick it out to the end of *carmen* 8; with the plaintive 'O me, that eye/Doth make my heart give to my tongue the lie,' on the contrary, Astrophil's resolve collapses in the couplet of

Sidneian Indirection

Sonnet 47, while the other poet's conduct serves to remind us that Astrophil might have behaved other than he did.

The device of the foil-text is of course a familiar one to students of the lyric cycle,[7] and to students of *Astrophil and Stella* in particular. Kalstone has for example analyzed the complex interplay between Sidney's 'Who will in fairest booke of Nature know' (Sonnet 71) and Petrarch's 'Chi vuol veder quantunque po Natura' (*Rime* 248), in which a re-evaluation of the whole of the later sonnet is eventually forced upon us by the divergence of '"But ah," Desire still cries, "give me some food"' from Petrarch's final verse, 'Ma se più tarda, avrà da pianger sempre.'[8] Referring in a recent essay to these lyrics and others, among them *Astrophil and Stella* 47, A.C. Hamilton distinguishes Sidney's handling of *innamoramento* and *commiato* from that of his model. And Roche's reading of the poem, which for the most part shares its doctrinal perspective with several persuasive essays by Sinfield,[9] naturally locates its foil-texts in Holy Scripture, and also in Plato and Ovid.

The point I would emphasize here concerns the ironies often inherent in what Kalstone describes as 'profound differences in attitude' (p. 118), in the gap that opens between Sidney's ostensible model and the details of Sidney's poem itself. For it seems increasingly clear that 'irony is the operative word' for us who explore 'the essential ambiguities of Sidney's writings.'[10] The notion more specifically of what may be termed 'ethical irony' can be expected for several reasons, I submit, to help clarify the ironic structure of *Astrophil and Stella*: first, at the same time as the term alludes to the attitudinal gap, the divergence in ethos, of which irony is often a function, it of course suggests the pervasive importance of the moral issues that preoccupy many such critics as Roche and Sinfield in their interpretation of the poem--'the ethic part . . . virtues or vices and the natures of passions,' as Sidney puts it in a letter to his brother Robert;[11] second, like the term 'dramatic irony,' which it inevitably (and intentionally) recalls, 'ethical irony' suggests the sort of pattern or structure that is by no means immediately accessible to the individual consciousness of a character or perhaps even to that of a more or less casual spectator; and last, the phrase seems to me to broaden our sense of Sidneian irony still further by recalling the old grammarian's term 'ethical dative' for such locutions as Bottom's memorable ' I will roar *you* as gently as any sucking dove,' Hotspur's '[he] cut *me* off the heads/Of all [the king's] favorites,' and (the to us perhaps more familiar use with a preposition) Sir Oliver Surface's 'There's a fellow *for you*--would you believe it!'[12]

To explain briefly, the ethical dative or 'dative of feeling' serves of course 'to imply that a person, other than the subject or object [of a sentence], has an indirect interest in the fact stated' (*OED*, s.v. *ethical*). Employed exclusively with pronouns and often essentially untranslatable when found in Greek and Latin (the Greek *toi* 'surely' is thought to be a petrified form of *soi* 'for you' in this sense), the ethical dative is 'often used . . . to secure the interest of the person spoken to . . . in an action or statement' and 'to introduce general statements or maxims.'[13] It thus serves to relate an individual in the loosest way, implicitly, by indirection, to the general circumstances of a situation, to an entire field of experience, as (to offer one final example) does Herodotus's broad-brush 'that's tyranny for you.'[14]

The characteristic irony of *Astrophil and Stella* results--much in the way of other Petrarchan cycles[15]--precisely from the divergence we find more and more evident between the actual conduct of Sidney's speaker, on the one hand, and on the other, the program either that Astrophil lays out for himself, or that is implicitly laid out for him by the innumerable details of the poem that delineate Astrophil's world, his field of experience, what one might call the ethical field of *Astrophil and Stella*. This, in Wayne Booth's phrase, is the limited 'world of discourse' of the poem,[16] what the new historian might perhaps be prepared to call its *mentalité caractéristique*, if not entirely *collective*, its reflection--itself inevitably partial--of the whole matrix of a stable culture.

Beyond the obvious fact of the Petrarchan precedent, how might we account for our poet's adopting an ironic structure for his work like the one sketched here, a structure that highlights ironic incongruity and partiality by reference to a broad and rich field of human experience? Not emulating his persona Astrophil, Sidney seems to have fully embraced a newly favorable attitude of his time towards that archetypal field-worker, Homer's Ulysses,[17] whose zeal to observe the manners and cities of men Hubert Languet admired in the young Sidney,[18] and whom Sidney in turn later urged as a model upon his brother Robert: 'Who travels with the eye of Ulysses,' Philip writes, 'doth take one of the most excellent ways of worldly wisdom,' and a little later he quotes the Homeric text (*Od.* I.3) in a fairly close version of its translation by Horace: 'Qui multorum hominum mores cognovit et urbes.'[19] He does so in the context of an extended moral and epistemological discussion emphasizing 'the mixed and correlative knowledge of things . . . which stand in the balancing of the one thing with the other.' Anticipating the opening sentences of *A Defence of Poetry* he reminds his brother, 'You that are a logician know that, as greatness of itself is a quantity, so yet the judgment of it, of might, riches, *et cetera*, stands in the predicament of relation.' And even when treating 'the other kind of knowledge,' that of 'things which are of themselves either simply good or simply evil,' Sidney tends to assimilate 'moral philosophy' to the Ulyssean model of moral anthropology. Then writing his friend Edward Denny in a very similar vein a year or two later in his recently discovered letter of 22 May 1580,[20] much as he would again write his brother some months after that, Sidney once more insists upon the particularity and the relativity of the individual understanding against the background of the general: 'For one thing is fit to be known by a scholar that will read in the schools and another by Ned Denny--and even in Ned Denny, one way to have been begone if you were a child and another of this age you now pass in.'

The letter to Denny proceeds to distinguish between this sort of knowledge, 'an outward application of ourselves,' and the essential Socratic virtue of self-knowledge.[21] This distinction, that roughly between '*prâxis*' and '*gnôsis*,' between 'well-doing and . . . well-knowing only,' as Sidney variously expresses it in the *Defence* (91.14, 832) both itself illuminates Astrophil's conduct and at the same time suggests a somewhat different means, still more germane to our present discussion, of assessing that conduct. For we are now principally concerned rather with Astrophil's manifold inadvertent failures of understanding than with his very largely conscious--if misguided--exploitation of a classic Augustinian incongruity: 'our erected wit maketh us to know what perfection is and yet our infected will keepeth us from reaching unto it' (79.25-26), or (in its Petrarchan formulation) 'et veggio 'l meglio et al peggior m'appiglio' (*Rime* 264.136). The uneven combat that Astrophil stages between reason and passion, after all, self-confessed time and again as in his celebrated 71st sonnet, openly shows at least the broad outlines of the *mentalité* from which it springs.[22] Therefore, essential to Sidney's poetic program though the attempt surely was to close the gap between *gnôsis* and *prâxis*, nevertheless our interest is perhaps even more profoundly challenged by the greater subtlety with which he treats those failures of understanding Astrophil betrays, failures that reflect the more exclusively epistemological gap which Montgomery suggests Sidney also considered it the function of poetry to attempt to narrow, 'a superior form of learning, leading to a knowledge we do not yet possess.'[23] Astrophil I think most fascinates us when he repeatedly exhibits just such a crucial insufficiency or partiality of understanding, when--in other words--he proves repeatedly inadequate to his dual vocation of poet and lover.

The few parallels drawn earlier between Sidney's work and that of the Roman elegists Propertius and Catullus serve to demonstrate how Sidney insists by ironic indirection on this apparent inability of Astrophil to understand the implications and likely consequences of his behavior. The field of Astrophil's experience, however, extends of course well beyond a familiarity with the Roman poets, or a familiarity indeed with the world of books in general. A network of significant detail of many different kinds, much of that detail--naturally enough--also essential to the subtle development of plot and character in the poem, functions to delineate the ethical field of *Astrophil and Stella* by contrast with which we see highlighted the diverse follies of Astrophil. For instance, let us again consider the issue of Stella's true place in the poem, an issue to which the callow Astrophil's preoccupation with his own passionate desire makes him largely insensitive. His audience may react otherwise. Sinfield, for one, argues that like Spenser's *Amoretti*, *Astrophil and Stella* clearly reflects 'the enhanced status conferred by protestantism upon marriage' and thus upon the woman herself in the love-relationship. Referring to Stella's as to Elizabeth's 'firm commitment to her true self,' he remarks aptly--though not without some oversimplification with regard in particular to Spenser's more conventionally Petrarchan sonnets--that 'what impresses Spenser frustrates Astrophil.'[24] Sidney, he writes elsewhere, 'establishes [Stella] for the reader as a standard of virtue against which to judge the speaker's manipulation and self-deception.'[25]

In *Poetic Presence and Illusion*,[26] Murray Krieger testifies by his readings of half a dozen sonnets in *Astrophil and Stella* to the both 'transcendent' and 'immanent' (p. 12) force of Stella's presence in the poem, to 'the present living reality of Stella as the absolute particular' (p. 17), as the object of perfect understanding, in such a sonnet as:

> What may words say, or what may words not say,
> Where truth it selfe must speake like flatterie?
> Within what bounds can one his liking stay,
> Where Nature doth with infinite agree?
>   What *Nestor's* counsell can my flames alay,
> Since Reason's selfe doth blow the cole in me?
> And ah what hope, that hope should once see day,
> Where *Cupid* is sworne page to Chastity?
> Honour is honour'd, that thou doest possesse
>   Him as thy slave, and now long needy Fame
>   Doth even grow rich, naming my *Stella's* name.
> Wit learnes in thee perfection to express,
>   Not thou by praise, but praise in thee is raisde:
>   It is a praise to praise, when thou art praisde
>
> (AS 35)

--a sonnet upon which Krieger dwells at length in summing up the pre-eminent claims he makes for the character named of course only second in the title of our poem. Indeed, if the force of Stella's *personality* inevitably makes itself felt later in the poem than does Astrophil's, nevertheless our sense of her personal presence develops by rapid stages once Astrophil addresses her directly in the climactic 'still I thinke of you' of Sonnet 30. Soon after this initial breakthrough, in the concluding tercet of Krieger's paradigmatic Sonnet 35, Astrophil repeatedly uses the familiar pronoun in addressing Stella, as will now be his regular, though by no means his invariable, practice[27]--and, one might add, a practice reminiscent of Petrarch's in the latter half of the *Rime*. For her part, far from being essentially unresponsive to Astrophil until shortly before the series of *basia* begins (perhaps until Sonnet 62 or still later), as Rudenstine argues, Stella early talks or sings to Astrophil, listens to him (perhaps weeping on one occasion), often argues with him, reads his work, and apparently blushes twice and expresses pity, love, and anger.[28]

Significant details like these suggest an increasingly intimate rapport between the title characters--Gentili writes of the partnership between them that develops from Sonnet 44 to Sonnet 85 (p. 153)--and such details thus contribute to an emotional movement also reminiscent of the later *Rime* in their frequently and increasingly deep tenderness. This movement culminates of course in Sidney's pivotal eighth song, rendering its action credible, most regrettable, and above all enormously poignant: 'therewith my song is broken' (104). We react as we do to the eighth song, I submit, at least in part because we have learned our way around the ethical field of *Astrophil and Stella*--and have done so by means often playful, ludic, but not therefore necessarily indeterminate as to their effect.[29] We consequently understand all too well what Astrophil is forfeiting, and why, and we also know that in his self-defeating passion, Astrophil himself understands very little of either.

It may be helpful to conclude with a second example of this latter sort, in which we again ultimately react as we do to Astrophil's conduct because it is incongruous with other conduct we have witnessed during the course of the poem--incongruous in this case with Astrophil's own earlier conduct. Warkentin, following Gentili, has recently remarked on Sidney's treatment of the theme of solitude in the dispersed group of sonnets, *Astrophil and Stella* 23, 27, 30, 54, and 104.[30] This group has several members in common with another memorially juxtaposed run of sonnets, in which Astrophil displays his disdainful reserve towards certain 'daintie wits' (3.1), 'curious wits' (23.1), 'busie wits' (30,12), 'luckie wits' (41.8), and finally 'envious wits' (104.1). The essential solitude Astrophil embraces in five Sonnets of these overlapping groups, 23, 27, 30, 41, and 54 (if we may exclude Sonnets 3 and, for the moment, 104), he most cherishes because it ensures the privacy of the lovers' microcosm, that autonomy of the world of two so dear to Jack Donne. Despite his earnest disclaimer of pride, 'Yet pride I thinke doth not my soule possesse,/Which lookes too oft in his unflattering glasse' (27.9-10), as Gentili points out (p. 266), Astrophil in fact prides himself on his inscrutability to *hoi polloi*, an inscrutability affording him protection not unlike that which in Catullus v and vii, it may be remarked, that poet vainly seeks against the kiss-counters.

Only Sonnet 104, common to both groups, occurs after the reversal of Song 8, and it itself marks a diametric reversal. Nichols, who would in effect count the friends of Sonnets 14 and 21, with their 'rubarb words' (14.5), 'right healthfull caustiks' (21.1), as being among the outsiders of the other sonnets I have listed, gives the gist of Sonnet 104: 'Even when his friends guess right, which they manage to do only near the end of the sequence, they are regarded as wrong to do so, because now they are stating the obvious.'[31] But the ironic play of similarity and difference goes well beyond this, in just the way it includes but also goes beyond our sense that, as Gentili suggests (p. 491), Astrophil's very admission here that he loves in itself virtually constitutes an act of impenitent pride. When at the end of the sonnet, Astrophil lashes out with 'Fooles, who doth it deny?'—when Astrophil so reverses his field, we catch the measure not only of his despair and pain, but of his own folly, folly committed both early and (even more significant) late.

This run of sonnets numbers one more at least, for in Astrophil's penultimate sonnet we inevitably recognize the same fools, and the same folly:

On servants' shame oft Maister's blame doth sit;
O let not fooles in me thy workes reprove,
And scorning say, 'See what it is to love'

(*AS* 107.12-14).

If his approach to *hoi polloi* has thus taken yet another turn against the background of the first half-dozen sonnets of this group, nevertheless Astrophil—even now a little smug—has obviously still not come to anything like a fully adequate understanding of Stella's role.

Much the same intricate movement, it can be argued, has also taken place at a late stage of Astrophil's long anti-Petrarchist campaign. As Sonnet 3 on the 'daintie wits' of course shows, and as Young argues by reference to Sonnet 92 (though not to Sonnet 104), the literary sonnets have significant links to those that have just been discussed; and in the first tercet of Sonnet 90, '*Stella* thinke not that I by verse seeke fame,' Young and Putzel find a clear repudiation of Astrophil's previously insistent claims of poetic originality, claims like that of Sonnet 74 in particular.[32] The most, however, that I think can be said for Sonnet 90 in this regard is that it suggests, but hardly asserts, such a repudiation—despite the tempting parallel from Shakespearean biography.[33] Characteristically, what we see here justifies neither Young's outright finding that Astrophil 'has discovered himself as part of the convention' (p. 88) nor Sinfield's equally polar 'yet Astrophil realizes nothing.'34 The ironies of *Astrophil and Stella*, though by no means vague, owe their force to a broad range of reference, and not to univocality or unilocality. The unity they possess they derive from the strong general coherence of an ethical field—a field cunningly patterned, if not in its great variety a wholly unified field—that ethical field against which the poet painstakingly highlights these ironies.

NOTES

1. Thomas P. Roche, Jr., '*Astrophil and Stella*: A Radical Reading,' summarized and discussed at the Sixteenth International Congress on Medieval Studies, Western Michigan University, 8 May 1981. See also Richard B. Young, '"English Petrarke": A Study of Sidney's *Astrophil and Stella*,' in *Three Studies in the Renaissance*, Yale Studies in English, vol. 138 (1958); Robert L. Montgomery, *Symmetry & Sense: The Poetry of Sir Philip Sidney* (1961); Neil L. Rudenstine, *Sidney's Poetic Development* (1967); Richard A. Lanham, '*Astrophil and Stella*: Pure and Impure Persuasion,' *ELR* 2 (1972), pp. 100-115; Germaine Warkentin, 'Sidney and the Supple Muse: Compositional Procedures in Some Sonnets of *Astrophil and Stella*,' *SLI* 15:1 (1982), pp. 37-48; Ann R. Howe, '*Astrophel and Stella*: "Why and How,' *SP* 61 (1964), pp. 150-69; David Kalstone, *Sidney's Poetry* (1965); Robert Kimbrough, *Sir Philip Sidney* (1971); J.G. Nichols, *The Poetry of Sir Philip Sidney* (1974); Alan Sinfield, 'Sexual Puns in *Astrophil and Stella*,' *EIC* 24 (1974), pp. 341-55, 'Astrophil's Self-Deception,' *EIC* 28 (1978), pp. 1-18, 'Sidney and Astrophil,' *SEL* 20 (1980), pp. 25-41; and William J. Kennedy, *Rhetorical Norms in Renaissance Literature* (1978), especially pp. 57-71, 206-07.

2.   'tandem te nostro referens iniuria lecto
      alterius clausis expulit e foribus?
namque ubi longa meae consumpsti tempora noctis,
      languidus exactis, ei mihi, sideribus?
o utinam talis perducas, improbe, noctes,
      me miseram qualis semper habere iubes!
nam modo purpureo fallebam stamine somnum,
      rursus et Orpheae carmine, fessa, lyrae;
interdum leuiter mecum deserta querebar
      externo longas saepe in amore moras:
dum me iucundis lapsam sopor impulit alis.
      illa fuit lacrimis ultima cura meis' (I.iii.35-46)

Translated by John Warden (Indianapolis, 1972). See James Finn Cotter, 'The "Baiser" Group in Sidney's *Astrophil and Stella*,' *TSLL*, 12 (1970), 381-403, for a study of the post-classical development of the theme of the kiss in its relationship to Sidney's poems.

3. Howe, 156, draws the parallel with *Troilus and Cris-*

eyde.

4. Max Putzel, ed., *Astrophil and Stella* (Garden City, N.Y., 1967); Richard C. McCoy, *Sir Philip Sidney: Rebellion in Arcadia* (New Brunswick, N.J., 1979), Ch. iii, especially p. 79.

5. Partial translation of v. 11 by Frank O. Copley (Ann Arbor, 1957).

6. In her edition of *Astrophil and Stella* (Bari, 1965), *ad loc.*, Vanna Gentili comments on the special dramatic qualities of Sonnet 47 and on those in particular of the verses in question. Subsequent references to 'Gentili' will be to this commentary.

7. See, e.g., Marguerite R. Waller, *Petrarch's Poetics and Literary History* (Amherst, 1980).

8. *Sidney's Poetry*, pp. 117-24, especially p. 119 and p. 117, n. 13. All quotations from the *Rime* conform to *Petrarch's Lyric Poems*, ed. and translated by Robert M. Durling (Cambridge, Mass., 1976).

9. 'The "Mine of Time": Time and Love in Sidney's *Astrophel and Stella*,' *Mosaic*, 13, No. 1 (1979), pp. 81-91; and see especially Sinfield's 'Astrophil's Self-Deception' and 'Sidney and Astrophil.'

10. Jan van Dorsten, review of *Sir Philip Sidney and the Poetics of Protestantism*, by Andrew D. Weiner (Minneapolis, 1978), *RQ*, 33 (1980), p. 468.

11. *The Prose Works of Sir Philip Sidney*, ed. by Albert Feuillerat (Cambridge, 1962), III, 131; Letter 42: 18 October 1580. All quotations from letters by Sidney are from volume III of this edition, but with spelling and punctuation normalized.

12. *MND* I.ii.75; *1H4* IV.iii.85-86; *School for Scandal* IV.ii (emphasis added).

13. Herbert Weir Smyth, *Greek Grammar*, revised by Gordon M. Messing (Cambridge, Mass., 1956), pp. 342-43.

14. V. 92ē; my free translation, after Smyth, p. 343.

15. See Robert M. Durling, *The Figure of the Poet in Renaissance Epic* (Cambridge, Mass., 1965), Ch. iii, especially pp. 73-76, and his Introduction to the *Rime*, especially pp. 20-22, for discussion of the basis of Petrarch's irony.

16. Wayne C. Booth, *A Rhetoric of Irony* (Chicago, 1974), e.g., p. 6.

17. See W.B. Stanford, *The Ulysses Theme*, 2nd ed. (Oxford, 1963), pp. 184, 296-99.

18. *Epistolae Politicae et Historicae Scriptae Quondam ad . . . Philippum Sydnaeum* (Frankfurt/Main, 1633), pp. 2, 34; Letters 1, 12: 22 September 1573, 28 January 1574.

19. After *Ep.* II.iii.142, also cf. *Ep.* I.ii.19-20; Letter 38 (n.d.), pp. 125-26 (all quoted passages).

20. John Buxton, 'An Elizabethan Reading-List: An Unpublished Letter from Sir Philip Sidney,' *TLS*, 24 March 1972, p. 344 (both quoted passages), also printed in James M. Osborn,

Young Philip Sidney (New Haven, 1972), pp. 537-40.

21. Cf. Dorothy Connell, *Sir Philip Sidney: The Maker's Mind* (Oxford, 1977), p. 10.

22. See Kimbrough's analysis of Sonnet 10 (*Sir Philip Sidney*, pp. 113-15), e.g., for the intricacies of finer detail that a similar sonnet can display.

23. Robert L. Montgomery, *The Reader's Eye: Studies in Didactic Literary Theory from Dante to Tasso* (Berkeley, 1979), p. 139; for a more general discussion of the importance for Sidney of the gap between understanding and conduct, see pp. 117-41, and also see Weiner, *Poetics of Protestantism*, especially pp. 34-50.

24 'Sidney and Astrophil,' pp. 32-4. See Louis L. Martz, 'The *Amoretti*: "Most Goodly Temperature,"' in *Form and Convention in the Poetry of Edmund Spenser*, ed. William Nelson (New York, 1961), pp. 146-68, especially pp. 154-61, for a discussion of the conventional sonnets that is notable for its sensitive treatment of the rôle played in a lyric cycle by apparent incongruity.

25. 'Astrophil's Self-Deception,' p. 12.

26. Baltimore, 1979, pp. 12-17. See also Ruth Stevenson, 'The Influence of Astrophil's Star,' *TSL*, 17 (1972), pp. 45-57.

27. For Astrophil's use of formal and informal second-person pronouns, see Ephim Fogel, 'The Personal References in the Fiction and Poetry of Sir Philip Sidney.' Diss. Ohio State 1958, pp. 333-34, and Putzel's note to Sonnet 30.14 (v. n. 4).

28. See Sonnets 36, 44, 45, 53, 57, 58, 61-63, 66, 67 and Rudenstine, *Sidney's Poetic Development*, pp. 247, 253-58, 262.

29. For the argument that in its playfulness, *Astrophil and Stella* exhibits 'a dynamic indeterminacy of effect' characteristic of Baroque art, see Gary F. Waller, 'Acts of Reading: The Production of Meaning in *Astrophil and Stella*,' *SLI*, 15, No. 1 (1982), pp. 23-35, especially pp. 30-32; see also Roger Kuin, 'All the Skill and Pain: Sidney and the Transformation of Medieval Tradition' (abstract), *SNew*, 1 (1980), p. 38.

30. 'Sidney and the Supple Muse,' p. 47; Gentili, especially pp. 266, 277, 343.

31. *The Poetry of Sir Philip Sidney*, pp. 97-98.

32. 'English Petrarke,' p. 83; Putzel (v. n. 4).

33. Cf. 'Without my plumes from others' wings I take' (11) with Robert Greene's notorious 'upstart Crow, beautified with our feathers,' *Greens, Groats-worth of Wit Bought with a Million of Repentaunce* (1596, STC 12246), sig. E3^v (1st ed., 1592).

34. 'Astrophil's Self-Deception,' p. 16.

. . . AND IN OURS

THE REWRITING OF PETRARCH: SIDNEY AND THE LANGUAGES OF
SIXTEENTH-CENTURY POETRY

Gary F. Waller

When we ask how we, in the late twentieth century, rewrite
the texts of Sidney and his works, we are also asking the
question of how Sidney rewrote the diversities and contradictions that made up the languages of his time. Traditionally,
scholars of Sidney and sixteenth-century English Petrarchanism generally have looked at the interconnections of Italian
and English Petrarchanism as 'literary' questions, and in
terms of those seemingly natural concepts of 'source,' 'influence' and 'allusion.' As Marion Campbell points out in a
later paper in this collection, such terms are increasingly
difficult to use unproblematically, and in this paper I want
to underline her argument by suggesting that 'literary' and
'cultural' texts are inseparable, and that a literary phenomenon like Petrarchanism is isolatable only at the risk of
vast oversimplification: any 'literary' movement is always
(indeed, always already) overdetermined, the product of a
complex, perhaps infinite, network of codes which continually
write and rewrite one another--the present tense of the last
clause being not a mere rhetorical gesture, but an indication
of the need to acknowledge that we always see what we term
the 'past' within our own history.
    Sidney's rewriting of Petrarchanism is an excellent test
case for examining what is, at root, a methodological question. Poor Petrarch's long deceased woes provided Sidney
with an extraordinarily hospitable discursive structure, the
power of which may be seen by his working within a set of
codes that had dominated European love poetry for over 200
years. Part of its power was that it was never, merely, a
poetical style and it allowed Sidney very easily to include
wider cultural as well as personal concerns. With *Astrophil
and Stella* and, indeed, English Petrarchanism in general, the
force of Petrarchanism was rewritten, in particular, by another dominant cultural language, that of Protestantism. The
combination of the two produces the peculiar strength of Sidney's poetry, and more generally, those curious Sidneian hy-
brids, the Protestant Petrarchan love-poetry of the Sidneys,

The Rewriting of Petrarch

Philip and Robert, Greville, Spenser and the Petrarchan religious lyrics of the Sidneys (this time Philip and Mary) and, eventually, the Sidneys' relation, George Herbert.

In this paper, I will focus on one issue in particular, which (given the curious history of criticism of *Astrophil and Stella*) is of particular relevance to Sidney studies. It looks, initially, like that old Burckhardtian commonplace concerning the place of the individual in the Renaissance but must, I believe, be formulated very differently, and that is the question of the subject, the 'I' of Petrarchanism. We are perhaps still used to seeing the Renaissance as the period in which 'individualism' becomes a pressing issue, and thus its poetry as demonstrating the centrality of the 'I' to our reading of the poetry and it is this assumption which I wish to reexamine. I will argue that in sixteenth-century England, Petrarchanism and Protestantism alike provided complex mechanisms whereby the desiring subject was permitted to speak, put under observation, and articulated in the presence and under the power of an Other (a mistress or a God), through which speaking wells up as a seemingly obligatory truth-bearing act and which asserts or desires to reveal a stable, given, pre-existent, autonomous and originating self. In a Burckhardtian view of the Renaissance, the category of the 'individual' or the 'self' is given; here I will argue that despite their reliance on the seemingly autonomous subject, especially as mediated through Christianity and radically reinforced by the Reformation, both Protestantism and Petrarchanism put into discourse a historically specific, radically decentered, self, one that finds its only recourse in language, that creates itself only as it is continually drawn into writing, and which discovers that the more it writes, the more it is in fact written, as words interpose themselves as frustrating and perpetually tantalizing yet always negative mediations between the anxious desiring subject and the object of his (or, though very rarely, her) desire.

Sidney criticism, as some of the essays in this collection show, is starting to pay attention to some of the ways recent insights into the way language works in culture can be used in literary criticism. I am thinking especially of the application of work by Foucault and Althusser, Bakhtin and Kristeva, and of the powerful work of Macherey--although, if we look back at more traditional work on the poetry of the sixteenth century, we may see how a work like John Stevens' *Music and Poetry in the Early Tudor Court* anticipates many of the points made about the interactions of social and aesthetic textuality by such recent writers as Richard McCoy, Arthur Marotti or Jacqueline Miller.[1]

I want to start with an observation made by Bakhtin and, in a slightly different context, by Kristeva. What Bakhtin called the dialogic nature of language--that one language always exists in relation to others--is perhaps most powerful in what we have traditionally privileged as the literary text. Languages interact, test or determine one another: in short, they rewrite one another, and do so, often, against their own intentions. Languages, to misuse Karl Marx's phrase, make history, but they do not always make it in the ways they intend. Particularly, Bakhtin argues on Rabelais, is this the case with the language of authoritarianism, the language of the dominant ideology of a particular social formation. Writing on the novel, Bakhtin notes how its language is 'a *system* of languages that mutually and ideologically interanimate each other. It is impossible to describe and analyze it as a single unitary language.' To this observation I would add Kristeva's Lacanian insight into the splitting of narration into the subject who speaks and the 'Other,' the subject who is addressed or is described in the narration --what she terms the subject of utterance. So where in Bakhtin, the combined languages of a text interact to produce a complex, ideologically contradictory text, in Kristeva, they likewise constitute the complexities and aporias of the speaking subject including, most importantly, the unconscious.[2] The result, in each case, is to call radically into question the notion of a finished, formally closed (or closable) text. Interestingly, Bakhtin tends to see poetry, as opposed to the novel, as tending to monoglossia, where the heart of my argument about the importance of Sidney's poetry for our understanding of sixteenth-century culture is that its greatness, its *energeia*, is precisely that it is the subject of a multiplicity of radically contradictory languages-- literary and social pressures, cultural as well as 'literary' languages. The forcefulness of Sidney's poetry arises from its failure to satisfy those needs and from its being under pressure of many contradictory systems of discourse, which struggle to master it, and in doing so, produce its characteristic energy. I see two of the major, though not the only, participants in this battle as Petrarchanism and Protestantism: at times they seem to reinforce each other, at other times and often in the same poem, they contradict and clash, tugging the poem in contradictory directions.

Let us start with Petrarchanism as the first of these two master codes, because it is clearly the more 'literary' of these two great discursive structures, and because, after all, it is as 'our English Petrarch' that Sidney's place in the conventional picture of literary history--Sidney in 'his' time--seems guaranteed. 'O Petrarke hed and prince of Poets all'[3]: thus Tottel introduced in the late fifteen forties what for the Elizabethan poets, though not most powerfully until Sidney started to work on *Astrophil and Stella* in the late 1570s, was to become an increasingly powerful literary space for any poet who had any pretension to being read and speaking in poetry. Indeed, if Elizabethan poetry is seen as made up of the traces and ruins of many texts, the single most powerful one is that of Petrarch. Throughout Europe for three centuries the emergence of what Foucault terms the writing of 'the truth of man's sex'[4] was mediated through Petrarchanism. Generations of imitators and commentaries elaborated a collective (mis)reading of his poetry of such power that it was impossible to avoid. Adaptability was a key factor in this power: Petrarchanism was called on to legitimate a seemingly neverendingly flexible rewriting of a basic trope of loss and desire. It provided a system of codes, a self-perpetuating language, which worked by persuading its readers that it offered insight into human love, but which owed its power precisely to its lack of fixed referentiality and its simply offering an infinitude of spaces for human subjects to insert themselves. From 300 years of *petrarchismo*, a composite mistress emerges, her physical characteristics the standard golden hair and black eyes (or their negatives), and so forth. Her most crucial characteristic was her icy or stony heart which inevitably caused the lover endless suffering and the desire, as Sidney's Astrophil voices, to endlessly 'paint' his woes. Typically the love relationship depicted with 'feeling pains' is a 'hell'--it is masochistic, articulated as cruelty, disease, distress, pain, the 'ungratefulness' of Sidney's 'With how sad steps, ô moone.' The effects of love are like fire, ice, blindness, paralysis, restlessness, helpless compulsion ('But yet, alas, how shall?'), and despite all his pain, the lover is drawn continuously onward, even while he puzzles over his self-torture and is teased by the mixture of his own 'truth' and the deviousness he seems inevitably drawn into. Desire is compulsion, repetition, frustration, disappointment and, above all, endless.

Thus Petrarchanism offered a poet like Sidney a discursive space to play in, to construct in effect a player (usually, almost inevitably, male) within a game, or playspace. It is a discourse that, moreover, seems to be referential, focussing on the depicting and idealizing of a real, unique, beloved, and creating a lover who offers patient, unrewarded but faithful, service. Stella is thus the quintessential Petrarchan lady in her (never forgetting that we see her through Astrophil's eyes) leading him on and yet never allowing him fulfilment; he is the man spurred on by his suffering, struggling to make 'some covenants,' to discipline his desire, occasionally jubilant in that he 'may say' that the 'she, deare she' is his, and yet never attaining what emerges as an unattainable, infinitely postponed goal. But neither 'Astrophil' nor 'Stella' is a function of the given discourse. She occupies the place not of a woman in a love relationship so much as that of the Lacanian Other--assigned a silent, iconic role notable primarily for her absence. She is the given gap in the discourse, an absence which is required for the poem in which 'she' appears to be written at all, and through which the absent but nonetheless determinative cultural pressures which shape the poem may enter. The lover's words arise and claim presence likewise only because of the absence they frustratingly seek and (as all readers of Sidney's poems observe) if the hoped for correspondence between word and desire were to be achieved or else finally and absolutely denied, then the sequence would end. Presence, achievement, indeed what we might term 'closure' of any kind, is not due to the poetry--there is no longer any urge to signify once presence, either positive or negative, is achieved. The much vaunted Petrarchan paradox is the primary acknowledgement of this continuing failure--that nothing can be achieved, willed into presence, without its opposite being, equally, 'true.' The Petrarchan paradoxes--the icy fire, the pleasant pain, illuminating darkness, joyful despair, whatever 'new tropes' for 'problems old'--always look as if they constitute a psychological code, especially when the poem's 'I' claims to represent or interpret 'actual experience,' but it is rather a structure of discourse which brings that 'I' into existence as a shifter, a necessary but neutral pronoun needed only for the poem to be written.

And here is perhaps the central characteristic of Petrarchanism and the one on which I would like to focus some attention. Not only does much discussion of the Renaissance lyric still focus on the naive biographical decoding of the 'I' ('did Sidney *really* love Penelope Rich?'), but even when we consider the 'I' in purely formalist terms, as a persona as the New Critics would have put it, or as a dramatic I, we still do not question that the coherence and unity of both poem and 'persona' are desirable and unquestionable. The 'I' thus becomes reified as a coherent voice or centrepoint of the poem's experience, a validating point of unity, the selfhood, if you like, of the poem itself. Now, what is at stake here is something far beyond fashions in criticism, the bickering between formalists and historicists, say--it is nothing less than the concept of the individual or unitary self that has, at least since Descartes, been at the center of the discursive and social structures of Western civilization. I am referring to the belief that the self, the unique person, is a given entity, a belief that developed within Graeco-Christian society into a belief in the person as an independent moral entity, both an agent and an immortal soul. Hegel, in *The Philisophy of History*, saw this development of the unquestioned centeredness of the subject as the destiny of the whole human race, and, moreover, something that made such cultures as the Chinese, who (it was argued) lacked the Western concept of the autonomous subject, frozen in their development.[5] Such an argument is of course not only spurious but a fascinating reflection on Hegel's own cultural presuppositions. Some of the most important recent discoveries on the functions of language within culture have, in fact,

The Rewriting of Petrarch

focussed on the ways this notion of the autonomous subject is brought into existence, demonstrating that the notion of the autonomous self and the concept of the unique 'person' are merely metaphysical, as is the corollary, that the self is a unitary, reflexive and directive source of consciousness. Thus when Foucault announces the 'death of man,' he is following in the footsteps of Nietzsche, Althusser and Lacan who have shown how the 'self' has been made problematic by so many of the philosophical, scientific and linguistic developments of the past century.[6] The self, like a literary text, is not a given, stable entity, but a site of struggle, fought over by conflicting languages, the most important of which are the changing socially constituted pressures of the cultural formation and the distinct psychic system or register, the unconscious. Subjects are not given but are produced by interpellation--the mechanism by which concrete historical individuals are constituted through the various cultural apparatuses and by what Lacan terms the 'Other' of the unconscious. Thus the subject is not a given or fixed object, but a site of conflict, a tissue, a weaving together, a production or practice in which a variety of selves emerge.[7]

Now, however momentous such ideas have become in past decades for our understanding of how we are constituted (put into the discourse of our whole social text, as it were), how do they affect our reading of Sidney? The late sixteenth century is one of those crucial periods in our history when the question of the 'self' became explicitly an issue of moment-- and it is in such seemingly peripheral cultural products as the Petrarchan lyric that the battle to establish a reified, universal given self can be seen gathering momentum. The Petrarchan 'I' is a device that puts into discourse two contradictory drives. One is an assertion of unity, of selfhood and consistency. This is the I of the speaking lover, that seemingly unquestionable unitary pronoun which opens Sidney's *Astrophil and Stella*, owning complex but identifiable feelings and urges with which he must deal, 'loving' as he asserts, 'in truth' and 'fain in verse' his love 'to show.' The other is the radically decentered self that the Petrarchan situation unfolds as an attempt is made to write itself into the world. 'I am not I, pity the tale of me' beseeches Astrophil at the end of Sonnet 52, and (ignoring the not irrelevant pun on 'tail') it is the never-ending tale that finds its only recourse in writing, in the perpetual dissemination of language that the Petrarchan situation unfolds. Petrarchan sequences have less to do with erotic impulses (however much they might be used as erotic stimuli--grasping Astrophil's tale, as it were); they are primarily part of a struggle to fix or create the self by means of language. The self that writes in the Petrarchan lyric is continually undermining itself--the more it writes, the more its words frustrate, the more it negates any desired congruence between, in Eugene

Vance's words, 'the spoken signifier and its signified, dispossessing both into a centerless, unending productivity.'[8] The longer the seemingly confident and autonomous self of the sequence pursues its goal, the less likely it will be materialized, and the less its signifiers point to some expressive or referential context--they point instead only to the discourse in which they begin and end. Not only does the desired woman of the Petrarchan lyric constantly recede--her primary function merely to frustrate the final, unreachable guarantee of the identity of the self which pursues her--but the very structures of the Petrarchan sonnet collections themselves are designed to express the impossibility of closure. Germaine Warkentin speaks of variety as the fundamental principle of the *rime sparse*; any sequential plot that may be suggested, by poet or protagonist, is primarily an occasion for rhetorical elaboration not discursive closure. Writing of the *Canzoniere*, John Freccero speaks of the Petrarchan sequence as 'fragments strung together like pearls on an invisible string,' always shifting ground, discontinuous, open to a multiplicity of juxtapositions and combinations, creating a self only as dislocated fragmentation.[9]

Something of the same point has been made by a number of commentators about the reading, the de-coding, of *Astrophil and Stella*. As I have argued elsewhere,[10] the Petrarchan sonnet collection offered a varied and complex discursive space in which not only the author might play, but also where readers could variously play, so that individual sonnets and collections alike provided opportunities for very different rewriting, adaptions to the particular sociocultural rituals or personal (or class-specific) tastes of its readers. The originating author, in this case Sidney, offers his poems to a varied audience of sympathetic listeners as a mirror less of his own experiences as of theirs. He becomes one reader among others as he contemplates the experience, listening and reading, thus producing what Barthes calls *ecriture*, 'writing.' Thus poems within the Petrarchan mode demand dialogue, argument, application. Wyatt's 'I wonder what she hath deserved' at the end of 'They fle from me' is a question thrust at its audience, and for completion of its meaning, the poem inevitably risks an infinitude of possible replies. Sidney's original audiences for *Astrophil and Stella* would likewise have given different, even though to a great extent class-specific, replies to the moral question posed by:

> Let *Virtue* have that Stella's self; yet thus,
> That Virtue but that body grant to us.

While all of Sidney's readers, then and now, share common activities in producing meanings, what is produced will, inevitably and infinitely, be different. The roles for the readers mapped out by the text are not coercive: even within

the courtly group among which Sidney wrote, the poems must
have variously seduced, tempted, stimulated, pleased, annoyed,
even bored. They demanded and demand, performance, not passivity. Their very life depends on our recognising that
they are loosed, disseminated, in the world and thus that the
lyric 'I' in itself is essentially inessential, anxious, longing for and never finding completion. It is what Paul Zumthor
has termed a 'hollow I,' needing to be filled, yet never
satisfied.[11]

Now I want to turn, as a means of illustrating my original methodological thesis, to the second of the great discursive structures into which Sidney was inserted--by belief,
class allegiance, and the conflicting pressures of his his-
tory--the revolutionary dynamic of Protestantism. Although
Sidney was, as Richard McCoy, Andrew Weiner, Alan Sinfield
and others have recently re-emphasized, a committed Protestant, nonetheless, as Macherey puts it, a writer is never in
control of the languages which write him; he struggles to
locate himself in the overlap of conflicting discourses which
he can never fully control or understand and which the reader
and critic must also struggle to tease out and struggle
with.[12] Sidney's writing is traversed by the conflicting
values and demands of Petrarchanism and Protestantism, and
between them these two great systems create in his work a
distinctive set of contradictions, focussing, in particular,
on the issue I have just raised, the nature of the speaking
'I' and the nature and status of the self. For Christianity,
the self, usually in its Greek philosophical rewritings as
the soul, is a given, capable of moral decision and judgement before God within the unfolding of God's providential
rule of history. And there is no doubt that it is Protestant
Christianity, with its distinctive theological and devotional
emphases, that gives English literature of the sixteenth
century a distinctive edge, and one far more significant cul-
turally than mere theological controversy would suggest. One
of the distinctive notes of sixteenth-century Protestantism
is an anxiety about the stability of the self, and the continuity of experience. It has often been pointed out how
wide-spread, indeed how obsessive, is the Reformation's
concern with temporality--it is an anxiety found in sermons,
tracts, and devotional works as well as in poetry. It is
articulated in Descartes' remark that 'from the fact that we
now are, it does not necessarily follow that we shall be a
moment afterwards, unless some cause, viz, that which first
produced us, shall . . . continually reproduce us.'[13] It has
often been demonstrated how Protestantism and especially
Calvinism, is a religion of panergism by which each moment is
upheld by continual, discrete intervention by God. One result
is that the devotional practices of the Reformation--and both
Catholic and Protestant share in this--are obsessively concerned with the self, and with the validation of a relation-

ship with God, with tests of salvation or repentance, with
searching for signs of grace, not as part of a collective
community, but on the level of the isolated individual,
through prayer, repentance, the searching of conscience, and
the reception of or resistance to, divine grace. It is a
self that is formed by a set of very concrete practices--not,
it should be emphasized, exclusively Protestant but codified
for most Elizabethans as Protestant and set out in those mag-
nificently logical, and appalling, treatises by Perkins or
Ames or Sibbes, and reinforced by the everyday religious
practices set out in the Prayerbook and the Psalter. The
self that is brought into play by the Reformation is one that
is anxious, obsessed with its status in the plan of salvation,
and in particular by the words by which it is brought into
confessing its anxieties. The post-Reformation world becomes
what Foucault terms a 'confessing society,'[14] fascinated with
developing techniques for producing the seeming truth of a
self in language, with exhibiting, explaining, reproducing
and sharing the intimacies of the self.

Now, just as in Petrarchanism there is an inbuilt contradiction between the hypostasized self and its endless dissemination in discourse, so in Protestantism we find an analogous
(more strictly, an homologous) contradiction. For Sidney,
these two great master codes reinforced each other's peculiar
anxieties beneath their obvious intellectual differences.
The much-debated question of how Sidney could 'resolve' the
conflict in his life and work between his courtly allegiances
and his religious beliefs may be resolved by considering the
structural problems they shared. Each is a discourse that
undermines itself at its most crucial point. Protestantism
demanded a total allegiance in every aspect of life; it created a stern, wrathful and all-determining god whose power
reached into every moment of a person's life and it focussed
relentlessly upon the inner coherence or disparateness of a
man's sense of self. So on the one hand, it is one assumption
of such a discourse that the self is given, immortal, prim-
ordial. And yet the self that is put into play in Protestant
cultural and religious practices is also not a replete but
an anxious self, one that is never sure that the next moment
will in fact be given. Protestantism is a religion of discontinuous grace, where each moment is created by the arbitrary and unquestioned *frait* of God, where continuity must be
continually held up by the new and discrete acts of God, who
calls each new moment into existence. The result is that what
Protestantism gave sixteenth-century England was a radically
insecure, anxious, discontinuous self--and I suggest that
part of the power of the age's poetry arises from this, and
in particular from the anxiety between the seemingly given
self and its operation. Stephen Greenblatt has pointed to the
characteristically anxious 'self-fashioning' of Renaissance
men, showing for instance, how a desperate faith in a central

self animates Wyatt's poetry, and that what emerges is the artificiality and despair with which that self is contracted.[15] Something similar constitutes, it might be argued, the very strength of Sidney's poetry--not to mention the *Arcadia*, which like *The Faerie Queene*, can be seen as a work that is not only unfinished but unfinishable, undermined the more it proceeds by the contradictions in the principles upon which it is built.

Where the unifying, fixed, originating self remains a fundamental assumption of both, nevertheless each in practice--poetry, devotions, everyday cultural practices of many kinds--continually contradicts itself and what each imposes is the fragility, artificiality and vulnerability of the self. In *Astrophil and Stella* (as in *Caelica*, or in Wyatt's or Donne's lyrics) we are in the presence of a continually decentered self that searches for fixity through the endless dissemination of language. It we look to other writers, outside of poetry, who were able to comment more explicitly on the process, we might look perhaps to Montaigne or Bruno, but it is a common *frisson* in much writing in the era. It is the anxiety that most Elizabethans labelled 'mutability,' that sense of being created by a world of arbitrary events, and having (though they did not see this) increasingly inadequate epistemological tools in which to express themselves. 'I describe not the essence,' writes Montaigne, 'but the passage,' and 'not a passage from age to age . . . but from day to day, from minute to minute to minute.'[16] These feelings echo throughout Elizabethan literature, religious and secular, as writers from the time of Sidney on wrestled with a residual and increasingly archaic metaphysical model within which to locate themselves. The 'I' of their poetry is an anxious 'I,' longing for a stable center, needing to be reassured and never satisfied, or satisfiable, its desire still crying out for food.

In investigating Sidney, the place of Protestantism as a complicating and contradicting factor is especially crucial. Yet it is odd how little recent work has been done on investigating the contribution of Protestantism's peculiar discursive *structures* (as opposed to its theology and devotional practices) to Sidney's work. Indeed, the place of Protestantism in accounts of sixteenth-century poetry generally remains largely confined to discussions of attacks on or suspicion of poetry, theater and the imagination and to the influence of Protestant theology. Recently, however, we have become attuned to what Barbara Lewalski has described as a substantial and complex Protestant poetics which produced a large and, until recently, neglected body of poetry. Much Protestant poetry, especially before the Sidneys took up the project of versifying the Psalms, is undeniably dull and undistinguished, interesting largely as examples of undisguised ideological propaganda, a simplistic and unsubtle attempt to render poetically memorable (or, given the monotony of its versification, *re-memorable*) a set of doctrinal positions, much perhaps in the style of the 1930s Soviet realism. But, nonetheless, it is there for our investigation and by the 1570s had certainly produced, in the Sidney psalms, one minor masterpiece and substantially contributed to one major work, Spenser's *The Faerie Queene*. Protestant lyric poetry, self-consciously competing with the profane love lyrics of the English *petrarchisti*, took as its model those parts of the Bible which were received as poetry, notably the *Psalms*--and thus David became the approved mirror of the Christian poet. It focussed on the inner life of the penitent or desiring Christian; on the anguished struggles of the Christian soul to put desire into language, to work through the paradoxes and impossibilities of meeting a beloved's demands, in this case an all-powerful, determinative God.

   Part of the curious history of criticism of *Astrophil and Stella* has been that of conflicting readings: Sidney has been depicted as articulating a courtly, sometimes neoplatonist, playfully Petrarchist 'vision,' on the one hand; on the other, his poems are seen as moralistic, Protestant *exempla*. In the era of positivist historicism or New Critical formalism, presumably such disagreement would have been seen as potentially decidable by the usual and seemingly natural process of formal analysis, historical research, and discussion. But analysis and research reveal a Sidney who is *both* Protestant and Courtly. More rewarding than finding a stable 'Sidney' somewhere 'behind' the poems is to trace the ways the poems are traversed by a variety of overlapping and contradictory discourses--a 'crossroads' as Ann Jones and Peter Stallybrass put it in their paper at the 1982 Sidney Conference in Waterloo, Canada.[17] But the 'undecidability' of Sidney's poems is not simply the undecidability of textuality so beloved by deconstruction. While it may be true that *Astrophil and Stella* is a powerful example of a collection of poems where contradictory codes force each other into strange shapes, nonetheless these contradictions are inseparable from the contradictory codes of his society--'literary' text is inextricably interwoven text. Sidney's poems--like his life as both courtier and Protestant patriot--are traversed by contradictory demands which gives them their characteristic energy. They bring into play both Protestant piety and courtly ambition; they confuse the codes of courtiership and piety, just as some of his sister's psalms undermine their own pious intentions by continual reference to courtly grace and sophistication, or Herbert's piety is contradicted by the flirtatiousness and eroticism of his courtly poetic.

   I commenced this paper by a methodological suggestion--that we should not, at the risk of gross simplification, separate out 'literary' from 'social' text in a consideration of Sidney in 'our' history or, for that matter, in 'his.'

The Rewriting of Petrarch

Neither Petrarchanism nor Protestantism is simply, respectively, a literary or religious phenomenon, and it is regrettable if we speak of them in isolation as if they did not coexist in the minds and practices of writers like Sidney. Frederic Jameson has pointed out that ideological change is often fought out within a set of explicit codes that may disguise the real historical issues at stake. What we traditionally have called Renaissance individualism, and described by Jacob Burckhardt as a central focus on the whole period, is not only at once being asserted *and* called into question by Petrarchanism, but by the revolutionary dynamics of the age, by Protestantism, even when clearly and explicitly it sought to reify the central significance of the individual soul before God. In *Keywords* Raymond Williams pointed out how between the fifteenth and seventeenth centuries the word 'individual' came to apply less to a person as a member of a community and more to a person as separate from the community. There are important ways Protestantism and Petrarchanism contributed to this change, but it should always be born in mind that we must not consider these two great codifications as abstract systems so much as convenient labels to describe shifting, overlapping, contradictory sites of struggle and debate. Jameson's advice in *The Political Unconscious*, 'Always historicize,' must be taken very seriously: treatments of English Petrarchan poetry, even when dressed up *as* literary history, have notoriously presented both as disembodied systems of ideas that somehow float around in a nebulous, abstract universe known by such a title as the 'Elizabethan world picture.'[18] Without wanting to fall into a Durkheimian or Weberian determinism, and reducing such contradictions directly to 'origins' in economic changes in late feudalism or early capitalism, nonetheless the contradictions I have been considering contribute to a complex set of interactions in the whole social formation. Any 'literary' work is not an abstract set of ideas but a material practice, and as John Stevens insists, grows out of and brings into play the tensions and demands of very precise social situations and concrete cultural practices. But of course, systems of ideas, the very term 'idea' itself, are conveniently reifiable labels and in treating the literary practices of any age so complex and contradictory as the Elizabethan, we must pay careful attention to the ways ideas are made to appear as if they were fixed, given, natural and thus removable from the flux and accidents of real history. As Macherey insists, the writer is not the autonomous producer of the materials he encodes: he may be the material agent of writing, but he is always situated within contradictions he cannot master, spoken by language within which he wrestles to locate himself--and the 'great' writer, if we want to use such a term, is precisely he whose writings reveal most actively the contradictions and strains of those languages. In Alan Sinfield's words, he can thus treat the literary text as an intense, 'particularizing pattern land across the changing grid of social possibilities granted by the cultural formation,' and so is subject like it to tension, antagonism and pressures which may not or only partially surface but which nonetheless bring it into being.[19]

When we read Sidney in the context of other sixteenth-century English poetry and mark the interactions of the great discursive systems which pressured it into being, we see what lies behind what Sidney termed *energeia*, the distinguishing mark of powerful writing--it is the product of a text's attempt to efface the struggles which have produced it. And the task of criticism becomes therefore that of bringing to life those struggles, of teasing out the discourses that fight within or in the vicinity of the text, marking the eloquent silences or half-silences, posing the questions of why the text is as it is, and of its necessary absences, where, as Macherey puts it, not only does the text not speak but where it cannot speak.[20]

One of the most powerful tools we have in the process is to put alongside the text those struggles which it has worked most energetically to suppress. In an ideologically charged literature like that of the Elizabethan period, these will often be political struggles, or political struggles masquerading as religious. Or it will involve asking what kinds of statements the age made possible or plausible to articulate and why--how, in short, the age's ideological struggles were resolved, and how certain alternatives were suppressed or marginalized. A dominant ideology inevitably wants to bully texts into coherence, to conceal those struggles, to force language into being the transparent conveyor of seemingly 'natural' meaning. That is why a consideration of Petrarchanism in relation to sixteenth-century poetry is not simply a literary exercise--it is asking how Petrarchanism reinforced or undermined the dominant, seemingly natural, categories of the ideology of the age. By recreating the battle which had been effaced we can sense something of the energy that informs this poetry while at the same time restoring it to a vital place in *our* history, since we ourselves are not merely traversed by equivalent struggles but because those struggles have made us precisely what we are.

In Alain Resnais' recent *Mon oncle D'Amérique*, a character announces that 'we are others': I suggest we amend that to 'we are others' languages.' To study the poetry of the sixteenth century is to study some of the ways we have in our history tried to avoid facing that we find ourselves only within the infinite play of discourse. The 'individual' which, with his nineteenth-century assumptions, Burckhardt naturally picked out as a central characteristic of Renaissance is revealed as fiction of unity, continually created to avoid acknowledging our decenteredness, our transitory locus within conflicting and waning structures of discourse. At any moment of speaking we are, in Foucault's words, already 'enveloped in words, borne way beyond all possible beginnings.'[21] We study the poetry of the sixteenth century because it gives us something of the ways we can struggle within the discourses that speak through us. In the late twentieth century, in *our* history, Sidney's works occupy an especially interesting place.

NOTES

1. John Stevens, *Music and Poetry in the Early Tudor Court* (London, 1961); McCoy, *Sir Philip Sidney*; Arthur Marotti, '"Love is not Love": Elizabethan Sonnet Sequences and the Social Order,' *ELH*, 49 (1982), pp. 396-428; see also the essay by Jacqueline Miller in the present volume.

2. Mikhail Bakhtin, *The Dialogic Imagination: Four Essays*, translated by Caryl Emerson and Michael Holyquist (Austin, 1981), p. 47; Julia Kristeva, 'Word, Dialogue, and Novel,' *Desire in Language: A Semiotic Approach to Literature and Art*, translated by Thomas Cora, Alice Jardine, and Leon Roudiez (New York, 1980), pp. 64-9; see also Carol M. Bové, 'The Text as Dialogue in Bakhtin and Kristeva,' *University of Ottawa Quarterly*, 53 (1980), p. 120.

3. *Tottel's Miscellany*, ed. Hyder Edward Rollins (revised edition, Cambridge, Mass., 1965), p. 213.

4. Michel Foucault, 'The History of Sexuality: Interview,' *Oxford Literary Review* 4.2 (1980), p. 3.

5. Paul Hirst, 'Ideology, Culture and Personality,' *Canadian Journal of Political and Social Theory*, 7.i-ii (1983), pp. 118-120.

6. Michel Foucault, *The Order of Things* (New York, 1970), p. 104.

7. For Lacan on the 'self,' see, e.g., 'Conferences aux Etats-Unis,' *Scilicet* 6-7 (1977), 49; Bové, p. 9.

8. Eugene Vance, 'Love's Concordance: The Poetics of Desire and the Joy of the Text,' *Diacritics* 5 (1975), p. 49.

9. Germaine Warkentin, '" Love's sweetest part, variety": Petrarch and the Curious Frame of the Renaissance Sonnet Sequence,' *Renaissance and Reformation* 11 (1975), pp. 14-23; John Freccero, 'The Fig Tree and the Laurel: Petrarch's Poetics,' *Diacritics* 5 (1975), p. 34.

10. See Gary F. Waller, 'Acts of Reading: the Production of Meaning in *Astrophil and Stella*,' *Studies in the Literary Imagination* 15 (1982), pp. 23-35; see Jacqueline Miller's essay in this collection for comments upon and qualifications of this approach.

11. Paul Zumthor, 'From the Universal to the Particular in Medieval Poetry,' *MLN*, 85 (1970), p. 816.

12. Pierre Macherey, *A Theory of Literary Production*, translated by Geoffrey Wall (London, 1978), pp. 57-8.

13. René Descartes, *Principles of Philosophy, A Discourse on Methods, etc.*, translated by John Veitch (London, 1912),

p. 173.

14. Michel Foucault, *The History of Sexuality: Vol. I--An Introduction*, translated by Robert Hurley (New York, 1978), p. 59.

15. Stephen Greenblatt, *Renaissance Self-Fashioning* (New Haven, 1979).

16. Michel de Montaigne, *Essays*, translated by John Florio, introduction by A.R. Waller (London, 1910), II, p. 232.

17. See 'Courtship and Courtiership: The Politics of Astrophil and Stella,' forthcoming in *SEL*.

18. Frederic Jameson, *The Political Unconscious* (Ithaca, 1981), pp. 84, 9; Raymond Williams, *Keywords* (London, 1976), pp. 133-6.

19. Macherey, p. 41; Alan Sinfield, *Literature in Protestant England 1560-1660* (London, 1983), p. 4.

UNENDING DESIRE: SIDNEY'S REINVENTION OF PETRARCHAN FORM
IN *ASTROPHIL AND STELLA*

Marion Campbell

The search for origins is a common and intelligible, but doomed, project, since our notions of where we come from depend on our sense of where we are, and the past is invariably constructed in the image of the present. In the field of literary studies, the concept of 'influence' provides a good example of this problem, and a convenient starting point for my argument. Traditional literary scholarship is so accustomed to tracing 'sources' and establishing lines of 'influence' that it is not often noticed how misleading these metaphors are. For the way in which we choose to talk about the relationship of the emitter and the receiver of influence neatly and surreptitiously inverts the power structure by casting the emitter as the active force and the receiver as merely passive. But of course we are dealing not with the passive reception but rather the active appropriation of material; as Richard Ellmann reminds us in another context '"influence" is a term which conceals and mitigates the guilty acquisitiveness of talent . . . . Writers move upon other writers not as genial successors but as violent expropriators.'[1] So it is clear that we can't just say that Petrarch was 'in the air,' blown north from the warm lands of Italy as a literal 'inspiration' for Sidney, who was striving to revitalise the dormant practice of English poetry. The question is rather why Sidney found Petrarchanism an appropriate model to express the political, social, and artistic tensions of the Elizabethan court. And in answering that, we need to consider what Sidney's notion of Petrarchanism might have been. This reveals a further problem with the concept of influence: namely, that it assumes in the source a single, unchanging and recoverable identity which can be used as a standard against which to judge or interpret the influenced text. But while it may be artistically appropriate or polemically convenient for writers to claim to have drunk from the 'pure well of Petrarch undefiled,' it is the business of critics to recognise that there is no monolithic interpretation of Petrarch. The history of the readings of Petrarch is at least as varied as the range of readings of Sidney that we are trying to use 'Petrarch' to arbitrate between. The category of 'influence,' then, is a device for constructing an originary meaning, a site of intelligibility, from which to constrain the interpretation of other texts--but that is an authority that it cannot claim legitimately. 'Influence' must be recognised not as an objective fact, nor an authoritative source of meaning, but as a critical method--and a contentious one at that.

What is at stake here is more than just a deconstructive quibble over the status of the metaphors we use to describe our critical activities. The interpretation of Renaissance literature has long been safeguarded by a seemingly impregnable historical scholarship. But recently, revisionist notions of literary history have begun radically to question the nature of the 'reality' that scholarship claims to be able to recover, and to show the inextricable dependence of the past and the present in the process of interpretation.[2] Literary history involves an understanding of how each author is continually rewriting the texts of his/her predecessors, and suggests that a perception of poetic relationships is crucial to the process of interpretation, which involves the synchronic interactions of texts as well as their diachronic progression. My position in this paper is that criticism is best concerned with establishing relationships or interactions between texts, instead of trying to define fixed entities or identities for poetic works. This process provides a paradigm not only for the relationship between literary texts, but between those texts and the critical discourse which interprets or constitutes them. Further, this model of interaction allows us to see a way of reconciling 'formalist' or 'generic' explanations of a text-in-itself with broader cultural or historical frames of reference, since we construct the text in the same way and using the same tools as we construct the larger cultural systems which the text defines and is defined by. So I am dealing with intertextuality (text in relation to other texts and to critical discourse) and what has been called intercontextuality (the contextualising of the production and interpretation of texts).

Sidney's *Astrophil and Stella* is conventionally regarded as a Petrarchan sonnet sequence. In an effort to examine what that label might mean, I want to look at a number of ways of reading Petrarch's *Canzoniere*, and suggest how these affect our understanding of Sidney's poem. My object is to establish a way of relating 'Petrarch' and 'Sidney' not in terms of any pseudo-historical flow of influence, nor by elevating an authoritative, single, closed interpretation of one poem as a yardstick for reading the other, but by bringing together two synchronically existing texts via the mediation of a critical method. Interpretation of *Astrophil and Stella* remains doggedly traditionalist; still produced primarily by biographical scholars, romantic expressivists, numerologists, persona theorists, it is thus tied to the critical methods of historical reconstruction or New Criticism. Recent accounts of the themes and form of Petrarch's poem seem to me more theoretically sophisticated than anything that Sidney studies have yet arrived at, and I believe that a reading of *Astrophil and Stella* could profit from the application of these methods. My own analysis of Sidney's poem draws on current readings of Petrarch to focus on the thematics of desire in *Astrophil and Stella* and to suggest how this relates to its poetics of fragmentation.

Astrophil and Stella manipulates a continuous parallel between the act of writing poetry and the act of making love. Sonnet 1 announces itself programatically as a persuasion to love and sets up an intimate connnection between the speaker as poet and lover. The second sonnet develops this thematic link, as well as establishing the possibility of sequentiality by its echoing of rhetorical structures from Sonnet 1; thus, the parallel between writing and loving is underlined rhetorically by the parallel construction of Sonnets 1 and 2. It further becomes clear that it is only the frustration of the poet's love which will keep the poem going. Consummation (the successful termination of the love affair) would remove the need for any further poetry writing, and thus close down the poem; unrequited love, paradoxically, is always a far more fruitful subject for poetry. So frustration fuels the poem, but it cannot terminate it; the event that would achieve that belongs to the realm of experience, not art. Astrophil writes his sonnets not simply to persuade Stella to return his love, but as a surrogate for the act of loving itself. The Petrarchan convention which Astrophil adopts forces a certain decorum on him, and provides him with a ready-made vocabulary of wooing. Key-words like 'pity' and 'grace' already bear a metaphorical weight, and need to be translated: the 'grace' that Astrophil desires is the sexual favours of his lady. Astrophil shows his awareness of the duality of the Petrarchan language which he is forced to adopt in Sonnet 2: 'I call it praise to suffer Tyrannie,' he says, in a fully self-conscious acceptance of Petrarchan diction, with its static oxymora and futilely repeated gestures. Astrophil is trying on the role of the Petrarchan lover; similarly, as poet, he is exploring how far those conventions can take him in articulating his emotions. In Sonnet 60 we are told:

> Now I, wit-beaten long by hardest Fate,
> So dull Am, that I cannot looke into
> The ground of this fierce *Love* and lovely hate:
> Then some good body tell me how I do,
>   Whose presence, absence, absence presence is;
>   Blist in my curse, and cursed in my blisse.

Those paradoxes--of love and hate, presence and absence, bliss and curse--define the area of experience which the Petrarchan convention investigates. It is the transforming power of love which allows a mediation between the opposed terms of the basic Petrarchan paradox: the *impasse* between the lady's cruelty (the Petrarchan way of talking about her chastity) and lover's desire. In Sonnet 57, the lady's voice 'so sweets my paines, that my paines me rejoyce'; in 44, again through the agency of song, 'the sobs of mine annoyes/Are metamorphosed straight to tunes of joyes.' The juxtaposition through rhyme of 'joyes' and 'annoyes' occurs many times in the sequence, as the sign of the metamorphic power of love and its control over the lover's emotions.

For Petrarch, the act of falling in love is a fragmentation of the personality, an emotional dispersal under the pressure of desire. This experience is expressed in fragments of verse or 'scattered rhymes':

> You who hear in scattered rhymes the sound of those
> sighs with
> which I nourished my heart during my first youthful
> error,
> when I was in part another man from what I am now.[3]

Here, at the opening of the *Canzoniere*, is announced the theme of the transformation of the self under the power of love: the lover is fragmented across time (separated from his past self) as well as being torn with conflicting emotions (vain hopes and vain sorrows). This psychological experience of fragmentation is from the beginning linked to the formal structure of the poems that describe it, suggesting how closely connected the making of verse is to the making of the self. This is the point of Petrarch's title for his collection: *rerum vulgarium fragmenta* (fragments of vernacular poetry), translated into Italian in the first poem as *rime sparse* (scattered rhymes). Petrarch's editor and translator Robert Durling speculates that this may be the first use of the term 'fragment' to describe a kind of work of art:

> For Petrarch the term expresses the intensely self-critical awareness that all integration of selves and texts is relative, temporary, threatened. They flow into multiplicity at the touch of time, their inconsistencies juxtaposed as the successive traces of a subject who dissolves and leaves only words behind.[4]

The parallel between text and self is maintained in the tension between unity and fragmentation, the dialectic established in the structure of the poem between scattering and integration. The mode which expresses this process is metamorphosis, a concept which mediates between theme and form, poem and source, unit and whole. Its dominant value is in the expression of the multiple changes of the self under the transforming power of love. But since Ovid, metamorphosis has been not only a psychological but also a literary concept; hence its particular usefulness in defining the relationship of later versions of Petrarchanism to their predecessors, and even more importantly, in understanding how the effect of sequence is created as one poem in a series transforms into the next. In its most general aspect, metamorphosis reflects the change of human, mutable, temporal experience into the eternal. The final form of Petrarch's 'scattered rhymes' is achieved only when human experience is seen from a divine perspective, and the fragments of the self are gathered into the eternal Book of God.

Sidney's investigation of the psychology of the lover also uses the dynamics of fragmentation, and may be elucidated in terms of the Petrarchan model that I have just sketched. Cupid is presented as the personification of Astrophil's love in a series of early and highly conventional sonnets, but the force of the device is to effect a separation between the lover and his love, to make it an independent emotion over which he has no rational control. The adoption of this particular mythological mode thus has important psychological value. It allows the human body to be seen as the battlefield for conflicting emotions or faculties, and it stresses the division rather than the integration of the body and the psyche. The heart is the traditional seat of Reason, but once it falls victim to Cupid it is given over to Passion--the debate between Reason and Passion inside the lover's body is the major theme of the first part of *Astrophil and Stella* (10,14,18). This self-division is the main form of fracture. Next in importance is the lover's divorce from the outside world, firstly seen in his separation from his friends and his loss of social identity. The debate between the lover and his own Reason is extended externally in poems where his friends assume the role of conscience and berate him for neglecting his public duties (14,21,23). A number of well-known sonnets show Astrophil engaged in performing some social duty but totally distracted by his concentration on his love (30,14, 53). Another dislocation which love effects is that between the lover and the natural world he inhabits. The traditional microcosmic relationship between the body of man and the body of the world is disrupted, as the lover sees in his environment not the signs of his harmonious connection with the cosmos, but a distorted reflection of his own emotional turmoil (31).

Sonnets 71 and 72 provide the climax of the debate between Wit and Will. Astrophil acknowledges the rational view of the relationship between Beauty, Virtue and Love, and the operation of the Platonic scale in which 'beautie draws the heart to love' and 'Vertue bends that love to good,' only to conclude with one of the most effective dramatic reversals in the whole collection: '"But ah," Desire still cries, "give me some food."' This objectification of Desire as a stark presence whose demands--although contrary to all the other motions of the lover's mind and soul--will not be stilled is developed in a more poignant and emotionally compelling mood in Sonnet 72, 'Desire, though thou my old companion art,' which begins as a farewell to Desire, clearly distinguished and yet inseparable from the speaker's 'pure love.' The lover believes that by identifying and separating his Desire he can eliminate it, but as the debate with himself develops he falls into the familiar habit of enumerating qualities--service, Honor, wonder, Fear, will, care, faith--and lapses into fragmentation. Desire could reunify him, because it 'wouldst have all,' but for that very reason it is banished. The emotional reversal comes this time in a simple half-line--'but yet alas how shall?'--that is eloquent of Astrophil's inescapable dilemma. He is doomed to fragmentation by a Desire that he is unable either to satisfy or eradicate. This conflict, and the tension between unity and fragmentation that it establishes, is central to the main concerns of *Astrophil and Stella*.

In contrast to, and as cause of, the lover's fragmentation stands the lady's inviolate unity. It is his knowledge of the correspondence between her beauty and her virtue that torments the lover and fragments him in the eternal battle between his Wit and Will. The strategy of the Petrarchan poet in this dilemma is to effect the final metamorphosis of the living woman into the work of art. By writing about his love, the poet creates a work of art whose beauty and permanence redeem the partiality and sensuality of human passion. This is the way that Petrarch's *Rime* develops: Laura is a distant inspiration, and there is no interaction between her and her lover. Even the name of the living girl becomes metamorphosed into the laurel ('lauro'), the reward of the poet, or into the breeze ('l'aura'), which is the poet's inspiration. So the *Rime* traces the process of the sublimation of human desire into heavenly love, a process helped by Laura's death (the ultimate absence). Through the operation of the creative power of memory, the completed poem comes to substitute for the unattainable woman.

How far does Sidney follow this process of sublimation? The name 'Stella' which labels the object of desire, has similar metaphoric potential to Laura. It is a suitable metaphor for the inaccessible lady, removed from the poem to the sphere of the heavens. The logical course for Astrophil is to reunify his scattered faculties by sublimating his desire in worship of the heavenly star, and shaping his poem to that end--that movement would make it complete. But Astrophil cannot accept the consequences of this metaphoric substitution: instead of allowing Stella's unity to appear in sublimated form as a star (beautiful, steadfast, unattainable), he wants to fragment her metonymically, to fetishise each part

of her body and enjoy her in fragmented fantasy. This is
what we find in the Tenth song, when the poet having been rejected conclusively by this lady retreats into solitary and
self-satisfying fantasy by visualising each part of her body.
This song attests to the continuing dominance of desire and
the refusal to sublimate it, and suggests that the poem is
doomed to remain unfinished as long as it pursues physical
consummation rather than the aesthetic satisfactions of formal completion.

Some support for this reading is found in the fact that
Sidney's most important divergence from the Petrarchan tradition is his stress on sexual desire. Sexual imagery dominates the first part of the collection; the pressure of desire
is explicitly acknowledged in the central poems (especially 71
and 72); the major action is the kiss, a metonymy for possession of the complete woman; there is increasing intimacy
between Astrophil and Stella, leading up to the crucial encounter in the Eighth song. But Stella consistently denies
Astrophil her body, which is thereby revealed as the only
thing he wants. Astrophil finds it difficult to maintain the
elevated Petrarchan rhetoric; instead of accepting the metaphor of the woman as inspiration, he comically wants to literalise it, and to be 'inspired' by her breath in a kiss.
In the group of celebratory sonnets following the stolen kiss
of the Second song, Astrophil continually proclaims 'My lips
are sweet, inspired with Stella's kisse' (74). The poetry is
not working to give the woman metaphorical significance, but
on the contrary, as an incantation to conjure up her presence,
bodily, in the verse. 'O absent presence Stella is not here,'
he cries in Sonnet 106, stressing the bald parallel between
her literal absence which is the source of his torment, and
her continuing presence as the subject of his poetry. It is
revealing that here the emphasis falls on her absence, as the
poet desires to incarnate her literally, not to substitute
poem for body. The absence of the woman, and the frustrated
action of the seduction, bring deadlock as the sonnets become
concerned increasingly with loss and absence. The sexual fantasy and release of the tenth song represent a dispersal of
Astrophil's erotic energies, previously concentrated on the
will to possess Stella. In Sonnet 91, he goes after other
women (unthinkable for a Petrarchan lover), making only the
perfunctory and conventional excuse that 'you in them I love.'
These poems show that sexual desire is still dominant, and
that it must find other ways of satisfaction if Stella is not
available; sublimation is not an issue here. The sequence
runs down after the rejection of the Eighth song as Astrophil
merely acts out a series of Petrarchan poses, trapped inside
a convention that no longer expresses any of the emotional
realities of his situation. *Astrophil and Stella* falters to
a stop in Sonnet 108 in the deadlock of despair, realised in
the final couplet:

That in my woes for thee thou art my joy,
And in my joyes for thee my only annoy.

The mechanical manipulation of this familiar rhyme reveals the potential sterility of Petrarchan paradox. The intricate connection of 'joy' and 'annoy' is no longer a fruitful metamorphosis under the power of love, but the sterile deadlock of despair.
 The account of *Astrophil and Stella* that I have offered involves more than just giving a new twist to the old theory of mimetic form (the form of *Astrophil and Stella* remains unconsummated because the desire that is its theme remains unsatisfied). It is a reading that attempts to establish a context for the poems; it resists turning them into a unified and completed artistic object by suggesting that they are directed to some extra-literary end, that they are instrumental rather than autonomous poetry. This distinction is related to the recent debate initiated by Richard Lanham over whether *Astrophil and Stella* is to be considered as 'pure' or 'impure' poetry.[5] These categories are taken from Kenneth Burke, who tells us that 'Pure persuasion involves the saying of something, not for an extra-verbal advantage to be got by the saying, but because of a satisfaction intrinsic to the saying.' This recognition that the poems may serve local or occasional ends relieves us of the necessity of identifying any single principle of unity, any consistent sense of self or continuing narrative, any transcendent interpretation for the sequence as a whole. And this remains true whether we are content to regard the subject-matter of the poems as sexual desire, or whether we wish to see sexual desire as a metaphor for political ambition, as recent criticism of the poem is beginning to do.[6] I don't have space here to consider in any detail the arguments about the social context of Elizabethan love poetry, but I want to indicate their relevance for my present concerns. The intersection of a literary text and a historical context is an issue that seems to be foregrounded insistently by *Astrophil and Stella*. The pressure of 'real' people and historical events is continually felt in these poems, and I suggest that this is one of the main reasons why it is difficult to identify literary structure or closure. The 'end' (ambiguously goal, object, destination, completion) is to be achieved not in the aesthetic sphere, but in personal, social, or political life. As Gary Waller has reminded us, these poems circulated in manuscript and are best seen as texts for performance, inserted into a specific context and gaining their full meaning from interaction with their audience.[7]
 This view of *Astrophil and Stella* as 'impure' or instrumental poetry, and the consequent necessity for reading it in a personal or social context, provides the first stage of my argument for the poem's resistance to closure. I now

want to examine more specifically the poem's form, and to suggest how recent formulations of Petrarch's 'poetics of fragmentation' may help us to analyse the structure of *Astrophil and Stella*. Sidney's collection of 108 sonnets and 11 songs is labelled conventionally a 'sonnet sequence,' but it is not at all clear what that term means, or what implications it has for the poem's form. The sonnet is a form which exhibits particularly strong closure and seems designed to detain its reader in admiration of its technical skill and ingenuity of thought and expression. When a series of such units is put together, juxtaposed spatially and temporally, the temptation to identify sequence (a sense of progression or coherence) is very strong. *Astrophil and Stella* offers itself to us as a formal unity in a number of ways (narrative, psychological, thematic, stylistic), but however much our expectations of closure may be satisfied in the case of individual sonnets or groups of sonnets, those expectations are defeated over the entire collection. The issue is seen at its starkest in the critical debate over whether we are dealing with a long narrative poem broken down into stanzas (quatorzains)--Alastair Fowler's position--or whether we have a collection of lyric moments strung together end on end, as C.S. Lewis insists.[8] But such polarisation of possibilities is not to the point: clearly the tension between smaller and larger units of formal organisation--between 'sonnet' and 'sequence'--is one of the major values of this mode of poetry. It holds out the promise of unity, but refuses to provide it. My own enumeration of perceived structures in *Astrophil and Stella* suggests that no single reading can account for all of the sonnets and songs grouped together under that title. Any interpretation which seeks a coherent unity will leave some loose ends; any individual reading will emphasise some elements at the expense of others, in a process replicated by the history of readings of the poem from the time of Nashe onwards. It seems clear, then, that any perception of a unified form for the collection is less likely to denote an inherent property of the text than a construction by a particular reader, influenced by his/her own historical position and critical fashions. Reading the poem involves us in a process of structuration, rather than leading to an apprehension of structure. To establish the significance of this conclusion for *Astrophil and Stella*, I want to return once more to Petrarch and his poststructuralist commentators.

In an important but frustratingly brief article on 'Petrarch's Poetics,' John Freccero sets out to define why Petrarch's poetic achievement should be regarded as revolutionary.[9] Dismissing the poet's thematics as banal and his verse forms as traditional, Freccero argues that 'the extraordinary innovation in the *Canzoniere* is rather to be found in what the verses leave unsaid, in the blank spaces separating these lyric "fragments," as they were called, from each other' (34). Freccero distinguishes two theories of language--an Augustinian view of language as desire, in which all signification is allegorical (all signs point to God, the only ultimate signified) and Petrarch's position in his poetry in praise of Laura (the lady who is the source of his poetic inspiration but also its final reward). This poetry denies referentiality and becomes auto-reflexive and autonomous. Freccero argues that this reification of the sign in an attempt to create poetic presence is the semiological meaning of idolatry: signs point to an absence and in that sense are allegorical, whereas idols (like fetishes) are a desperate attempt to render presence. The consequence of fetishisation is the fragmentation of the woman; the consequence of idolatry (of treating a signifier as an absolute) is the fragmentation of the text: 'without a principle of intelligibility, an interpretant, a collection of signs threatens to break down into its component parts' (38-39). Thus, the Petrarchan sequence may counterfeit the creation of a poetic persona or the development of a narrative through the physical proximity of the lyrics and their repetition of verbal and formal patterns, but this will remain an illusion, 'the product of the reader's imagination as much as of the poet's craft' (34).

There are a number of elements here that are relevant to a reading of Sidney. The idea that a collection of sonnets and songs without the traditional prose links--Petrarch's innovation--is inevitably fragmented, since the reader must provide the connections and fill in the gaps, is a more general formulation of our empirical observation about the proliferation of perceived structures in *Astrophil and Stella*. We have already noted that the thematics of desire led to a fragmentation of the lover, and the subsequent fetishisation and fragmentation of the woman; moreover, the absence of the woman from the poem is the cause of the lover's frustration and the poem's incompletion. Language, the poet's medium, functions in an attempt to render absence present by elevating a signifier to the status of a signified, by (literally) embodying Stella in verse. This stratagem is unsuccessful since Astrophil is not interested in substituting semiological for sexual desire; but for Sidney as poet it results in the fragmentation of the body of his text because he refuses to elevate any single 'principle of intelligibility,' as Freccero puts it. No consistent psychological or narrative structure can be identified in *Astrophil and Stella* because the poem (like Petrarch's *Canzoniere*) dramatises the process of creating a self and of narrating that self's history without those processes **ever** crystallising into the product of a self created or a story told. That is why the form of the poem is best seen as dynamic rather than static, metamorphosing as we read into an endless variety of forms, fragmenting and reforming, never achieving fixity. The poem offers us structuring elements in abundance, but these are included within its overall design rather than becoming the total explanation of it. It is the sense of incompleteness which is the persistent element in the pattern.[10] To see fragmentation as a principle of structuration provides a means of connecting thematics and poetics. *Astrophil and Stella* is fragmented because, under the pressure of desire, it refuses any transcendent unifying interpretation, any ultimate signified, while nevertheless involving us in the process of interpreting, the play of signification. For an age that has been taught about the erotics of the text, 'desire' labels not only Sidney's theme but also his relationship to his material and his medium. And since desire must always remain unfulfilled, the end of the poem is constantly displaced or deferred in a succession of readings or reinventions (Sidney's reinvention of Petrarchan form and our own reinvention of both Petrarch and Sidney under the pressure of our particular historical and critical positions).

NOTES

1. Richard Ellmann, *Eminent Domain* (New York, 1967), p. 3.
2. See Michael McCanles, 'The Authentic Discourse of the Renaissance,' *Diacritics*, 10 (March 1980), pp. 77-87.
3. All quotations from the *Canzoniere* are taken from *Petrarch's Lyric Poems: The Rime Sparse and Other Lyrics*, translated and edited by Robert M. Durling (Cambridge, Mass., 1976.
4. Durling, p. 26.
5. Richard A. Lanham, *Astrophil and Stella*: 'Pure and Impure Persuasion,' *English Literary Renaissance*, 2 (1972), pp. 100-15.
6. See Arthur F. Marotti, '"Love is not Love": Elizabethan Sonnet Sequences and the Social Order,' *ELH*, 49 (1982), pp. 396-428.
7. Gary F. Waller, 'Acts of Reading: The Production of Meaning in *Astrophil and Stella*,' *Studies in the Literary Imagination*, 15 (1982), pp. 25-35.
8. Alastair Fowler, *Triumphal Forms: Structural Patterns in Elizabethan Poetry* (Cambridge, 1970), pp. 174-80; C.S. Lewis, *English Literature in the Sixteenth Century* (London, 1954), pp. 327-30.
9. John Freccero, 'The Fig Tree and the Laurel: Petrarch's Poetics,' *Diacritics*, 5 (Spring 1975), pp. 34-40.
10. See Marguerite R. Waller, *Petrarch's Poetics and Literary History* (Amherst, 1980).

'WHAT MAY WORDS SAY': THE LIMITS OF LANGUAGE IN *ASTROPHIL AND STELLA*

Jacqueline T. Miller

At the beginning of Sonnet 35, Astrophil asks, 'What may words say, or what may words not say,/Where truth it selfe must speake like flatterie?' Although Astrophil often seems concerned primarily with flattery in the guise of truth, or truth in the service of flattery, the Sidney behind Astrophil may take the question more seriously. What is the relationship between language and truth? Can words reflect, manifest, or convey intention? Furthermore, if language cannot proclaim the truth without sounding false or hollow (like flattery), does the speaker have any control over his words--over what his words say and what they don't say? The paired questions of the opening line of Sonnet 35 suggest first that words can 'say' nothing, and secondly that words can 'say' everything and anything--and that there really is no difference between those two statements. It seems as though Astrophil has discovered that, despite the Muse's instruction in Sonnet 1, there is a possibly unbridgeable distance between 'loving in truth' and showing that love 'in verse.'

Murray Krieger has recently suggested that Renaissance poets, among them Sidney in particular, confront 'the emptiness of words as signifiers--their distance from their signifieds' and 'can accept words as insubstantial entities existing on their own, not to be confounded with their signifieds.' Yet he also suggests that the poet's struggle with the emptiness of words is resolved by 'use of a verbal analogy to the divine miracle in order to fill those words with substance,' a resolution that is accompanied by the poet's awareness of its 'merely verbal and illusory nature.' According to Krieger, in 'many of the best of Sidney's sonnets,' 'the poet's struggle with the emptiness of language and of poetic conventions is transformed and resolved as her [Stella's] transcendent power becomes immanent.' Once the poem 'manages to encompass her *being*, the breakthrough beyond the failures of language and poetic convention is achieved.'[1] Although I am in complete agreement with Krieger's analysis of the struggle with language that Renaissance poets engage in (one that, as he notes, is far more modern than we normally associate with Renaissance writers), I am less convinced by his claim for resolution, however qualified it is by the idea of 'willful illusion,' because he ignores a concomitant difficulty it raises. I have suggested in another article (and in a different context) that the woman in the sixteenth century sonnets is presented not only as a source of the poet's art, but also as a threat to it, requiring a complex strategy of negotiation between surrender and assertion of poetic autonomy and identity on the part of the poet/lover. Although Krieger discusses the way that Stella's presence in the poems can turn 'words against themselves' and reveal 'the bankruptcy of language,' he concludes nevertheless that through Stella 'a world of empty words is reconstituted.' What I would like to propose here is that in the sonnets that confront the emptiness of words, Stella is invoked not so much to transcend the problems of language as to highlight them. When Krieger describes the 'resolution produced by Stella's presence' as the poem's creation of its goddess, who in turn converts all its elements into her own, thereby bestowing new meanings upon them,' he is, I would suggest, describing a problem the poet delineates, not simply a resolution.[2]

In *Astrophil and Stella*, the emphasis on the indeterminacy of words, their lack of fixed points of reference, is often portrayed through the speaker's inability to enforce any single meaning on his language, and this is usually depicted through Stella's presence in the poems as their reader. Sonnet 44, for example, begins with what seems to be a radical departure from Sonnet 35; Astrophil claims that his words do effectively say what he means--they voice his personal truth. 'My words I know do well set forth my mind,' he begins, with assurance. Yet it quickly becomes clear that this, by itself, is no achievement, as Astrophil proceeds to consider the dilemma that these words do not have the expected or intended effect on Stella:

> My words I know do well set forth my mind,
>   My mind bemones his sense of inward smart;
>   Such smart may pitie claime of any hart,
> Her heart, sweete heart, is of no Tygre's kind·
> And yet she heares, yet I no pitty find;
>   But more I crie, lesse grace she doth impart,
>   Alas, what cause is there so overthwart,
> That Noblenesse it selfe makes thus unkind?

The conclusion he reaches, the only one available, is that these words do not communicate themselves to Stella; when his words reach Stella's ears, her 'heav'nly nature' transforms them:

> I much do guesse, yet find no truth save this,

> That when the breath of my complaints doth tuch
> Those daintie dores unto the Court of blisse,
> The heav'nly nature of that place is such,
> > That once come there, the sobs of mine annoyes
> > Are metamorphosd straight to tunes of joyes.

Stella does not respond to the woe that his words set forth so well, because she metamorphoses them into words of joy. Once his words are spoken, they become a part of the public domain, so to speak, subject to new meanings under the informing influence of others; and their efficacy is limited (he gets no pity from Stella) because he cannot limit their meaning.

Astrophil takes this a step further in Sonnet 57, where he recounts how 'The thorowest words, fit the woe's selfe to grone,' were sought and found, and then set off,

> Hoping that when they might find *Stella* alone,
> Before she could prepare to be unkind,
> Her soul, arm'd but with such a dainty rind,
> Should soone be pierc'd with sharpnesse of the mone.

Stella, we are told, 'heard my plaints,' and then '(so sweete she is)' began to 'sweetly sing' them, in the process 'making woe's darknesse cleare.' The poet concludes by describing the surprising outcome of his careful planning:

> A prety case! I hoped her to bring
> To feele my griefes, and she with face and voice
> So sweets my paines, that my paines me rejoyce.

Again, intention is thwarted--the 'thorowest words,' chosen to communicate his grief to Stella, turn back upon him and upon themselves. Stella infuses them with a sweetness that is her own (and that apparently empties them of, or at least obscures, his woe) and thus transforms the impact of his words so radically that the speaker ends up enjoying the recital of his own sorrow--in short, the very thing he hoped to prevent Stella from doing in the first place by finding 'fit' words to make her 'feele my griefes.' In each of these poems, it is precisely through an invocation of Stella 'who in turn converts all its elements into her own, thereby bestowing new meaning upon them,' that the poet figures forth his difficulty with language.[3]

Gary Waller has directed our attention to the way *Astrophil and Stella* emphasizes 'the inventive role of the spectator or reader who becomes an actor, a producer of the work's meaning'; however, he also seems to neglect a crucial area of poetic tension when he claims that the sonnet sequence 'encourages its readers to take unusually active roles in the assembling of meaning . . . by insisting at points that each reader bring his or her preconceptions, aesthetic and socio-

cultural, to bear on the poems.' Waller's essay is based on
the premise that 'always the most important audiences' of the
sonnets are 'the ones unnamed'--i.e., their contemporary
courtly readers and their future readers throughout history--
and although he speaks of the diversity of their possible responses to the sonnets, including disapproval and disagreement, he three times in his essay refers to this composite
audience as 'sympathetic.' Yet, although Waller mentions
Penelope Rich as a possible member of the original audience
of *Astrophil and Stella*, he to a large extent ignores the intended audience invoked within the framework and fiction of
the sequence itself: Stella. This is not to say that Sidney
did not have his larger audience of readers in mind, but
Stella cannot be dismissed.[4] The poet's plan, as described
in Sonnet 1, is, as Neil Rudenstine writes, that 'she must
be made to see her lover's plight, to feel what he feels, and
to respond with sympathy.'[5] And Sidney's comments on love
poetry in the *Apology*, that 'truly many of such writings as
come under the banner of unresistable love, if I were a mistress, would never persuade me they were in love' (*Misc.
Prose*, 116.35-117.2), suggests that, as Hallett Smith notes,
'the first consideration in love poetry' is the 'efficacy of
the verse from the assumed point of view of the mistress.'[6]
Once Stella's position as defined by the poem is recognized,
we may, I think, see that while the sequence may acknowledge
that its reader takes an unusually active role in the assembling of meaning, it does not necessarily encourage this--at
least, not without reservations. It is, in fact, precisely
the open-ended nature of his language and his poems--the fact
that his (named) reader will create her own meaning--that is
a source of constant frustration for Astrophil--particularly
because the audience he represents within his poetry is not
a sympathetic one. While Sidney does have Astrophil confront
the fact that *his* most important reader will produce her own
reading of the text, this is presented as a puzzling, baffling
situation that subverts the poet/lover's intention. The text
may never, as Waller claims, compel us into meaning, but the
poet within the poem finds it difficult to accept and deal
with this. Sidney uses Stella's role as audience and Astrophil's as poet to display, I think, his own uneasiness about
what Waller calls the 'reciprocity' that exists between readers and writers.

For Sidney in the *Apology*, the emphasis on the reader is
obvious, yet not unambiguous. Certainly, it is upon poetry's
effect upon its audience ('moving') that his claim for the
poet's superiority to the historian and the philosopher is
founded. Yet whether the poet should or can control that
effect is a more problematic issue. In her astute analysis of
this aspect of the *Apology*, Margaret Ferguson has suggested
that the problem for Sidney is that 'a written medium implies
a *reader* who perhaps cannot (or will not) understand his words

at all'; and his 'allegorical intention [the 'winning of the mind from wickedness to virtue'] does not exist until it is confirmed by the reader.'[7] In his famous reference to Xenophon, for example, Sidney reveals the importance of the audience to his poetic, and, in fact, the dependence of his poetic on the audience. When the poet ranges 'within the zodiac of his own wit' to produce a golden world, he does not simply 'build castles in the air'--he works 'substantially,' 'not only to make a Cyrus . . . but to bestow a Cyrus upon the world to make many Cyruses, *if they will learn aright why and how that maker made him*' (*Misc. Prose*, 79.12-5). The poet's success, in other words, is contingent upon the audience's desire and ability to understand both his intention (why) and method (how). Yet while the 'if' in the above statement gives the reader an essential role to play in the completion of the poem's function, it also recognizes the possibility that some readers will not fill this role properly, and testifies, as A. Leigh DeNeef notes, 'to Sidney's uneasiness over the notion of right readers.' Indeed, Sidney implies, both in his discussion of *mysomousoi* and in his discussion of how poetry can be abused, the existence of readers who fail to read it correctly or 'aright.'[8] Moreover, when Sidney explains (in freeing the poet from the charge of lying) that readers 'shall use the narration but as an imaginative ground-plot of a profitable invention' (*Misc. Prose*, 103.15-6), he does not make a direct claim that the artist's informing fore-conceit or idea can structure or determine that response. As Ronald Levao suggests, '"Invention" carries its full ambiguity here, and we cannot tell whether readers come upon a preestablished meaning or simply create their own. . . . We are not guaranteed a fixed unity between speaker and hearer.'[9] Hence Sidney faces a dilemma: his idea of 'moving' is based upon the premise of active readers, but this is a premise that provides the possibility of false readings and bad readers. The very thing that proves poetry's superiority and constitutes its power and purpose is the same thing that can subvert its ends.

A curious phrase in the *Apology* may sum up Sidney's attitude towards this: 'For Poesy must not be drawn by the ears,' he writes; 'it must be gently led, or rather it must lead' (111.28-9).[10] Sidney makes this statement in the context of acknowledging at least the partial validity of the adage, '*orator fit, poeta nascitur*' (although it is greatly qualified by the point he is moving towards, that 'the highest-flying wit [must] have a Daedalus to guide him'). While referring to the qualities of the poet and his process of 'making,' this statement recalls earlier comments about the function of poetry and its effect on its audience: 'the final end,' he claims, 'is to lead and draw us to as high a perfection as our degenerate souls . . . can be capable of' (82.14-6). 'Drawing' and 'leading' throughout the *Apology*, are words that usually refer to the poet's effect on his readers, not to how the poet creates, the relation of the poet to his poem. The phrase 'drawn by the ears' is not usually glossed by editors, but it yields interesting resonances if we consider the possibility that it may be an allusion to the emblem of Hercules (explained by Lucian in his *Heracles*, and referred to by writers like Puttenham and Wilson) with chains of gold extending from his tongue and attached to the ears of the people whom he is leading, to show the force of eloquence. Wilson sees it as an example of the power of persuasion:

> . . . such force hath the tongue, and such is the power of Eloquence and reason, that most men are forced, even to yeeld in that which most standeth against their will. And therefore the Poets doe feine, that *Hercules* beeing a man of great wisdome, had all men lincked together by the eares in a chaine, to drawe them and leade them even as he lusted. For his witte was so great, his tongue so eloquent, and his experience such, that no one man was able to withstande his reason, but every one was rather driven to doe that which he would, and to will that which he did: agreeing to his advise both in word and worke in all that ever they were able.

Puttenham provides a similar gloss:

> . . . they had figured an lustie old man with a long chayne tyed by one end at his tong, by the other end at the peoples eares, who stood a farre of and seemed to be drawn to him by the force of that chayne fastned to his tong, as who would say, by force of his perswasions.

And Puttenham concludes this chapter of *The Arte of English Poesie* with the statement that,

> . . . good perswasion is no lesse requisite then speache it selfe: for in great purpose to speake and not to be able or likely to perswade, is a vayne thing.[11]

Given this implied allusion, which would, it seems, have been recognizable to Sidney's readers, we may suppose that the tentative waffling of the statement that 'Poesy must not be drawn by the ears; it must be gently led, or rather it must lead,' may be of significance not only in relation to its specific context regarding the place of genius and inspiration in the poetic enterprise; it may also reveal Sidney's own ambivalence about and difficulty in determining whether and how much the poet should draw his audience, or be drawn by it; and whether this drawing (by whomever it is accomplished) is done forci-

The Limits of Language

bly, or 'gently.' That this is an issue in *Astrophil and Stella* as well as in the *Apology* (and that Sidney was as familiar with the emblem of Hercules as his contemporaries were) is revealed in Sonnet 58:

> Doubt there hath bene, when with his golden chaine
> The Oratour so farre men's harts doth bind,
> That no pace else their guided steps can find,
> But as he them more short or slacke doth raine,
> Whether with words this soveraignty he gaine,
>   Cloth'd with fine tropes, with strongest reasons lin'd
>   Or else pronouncing grace, wherewith his mind
> Prints his owne lively forme in rudest braine.

The opening reference to the image of Herculean eloquence affirms the power of the 'orator' to guide and lead his audience, which is so bound that even the pace of its footsteps is controlled by the speaker who reigns by holding the rein.12 But Astrophil raises a question about the source of this power, acknowledging a 'doubt' about whether the 'words' of the speaker or his 'pronouncing grace' constitute and confer this 'soveraignty.' 'Pronouncing grace' need not, I think, be confined here to a narrow meaning of 'delivery,' as some editors have suggested.13 The phrase that follows it, 'wherewith his mind/Prints his owne lively forme in rudest braine,' associates it with the 'true lively knowledge' that Sidney in the *Apology* claims poetry alone can provide when the poet 'yieldeth to the powers of the mind an image of that whereof the philosopher bestoweth but a wordish description, which doth neither strike, pierce, nor possess the sight of the soul so much as that other doth' (85.26-8). It is, as Geoffrey Shepherd notes, 'the setting out of a direct communication of a certain vision of truth,' and as such recalls Sidney's comments on 'that lyrical kind of songs and sonnets' in the *Apology*, and his insistence on 'that same forcibleness or *energeia*' that is the key to persuasion, needed if writers are to convince their ladies 'that in truth they feel those passions' (117.7). And *energia*, as Shepherd explains, 'is the power of presenting the subject matter clearly, and refers not to the words used in presenting the subject but to the vivid mental apprehension of things themselves.'14 Given these associations, we may then predict Astrophil's resolution to the doubt he has raised. He offers it in the final lines of the sonnet, but not without some surprises:

> Now judge by this: in piercing phrases late,
>   Th'anatomy of all my woes I wrate,
> *Stella*'s sweete breath the same to me did reed.
> O voice, ô face, maugre my speeche's might,
>   Which wooed wo, most ravishing delight
> Even those sad words even in sad me did breed.

The Limits of Language

It is obvious that 'pronouncing grace' (both as delivery and in its larger context) wins out over 'words,' but the answer to the question of how one can move even the 'rudest braine' has serious ramifications. There is a crucial shift of focus here. Initially we think we are being asked to judge on the basis of how Astrophil's 'piercing phrases' affected Stella. Yet ultimately we are asked to judge on the basis of how Stella's rendering (or reading, to use his word) of Astrophil's words affected Astrophil himself. In other words, the issue, though introduced as a debate over which aspect of a single speaker provides his sovereignty over his audience, is 'resolved' by setting into motion a competition between the speaker and his audience. In fact, by the end of the poem, the speaker has become the audience; and the audience has become the speaker with sovereignty, leading the original speaker. This is possible because the first speaker (Astrophil) cannot maintain control over what his words say; despite his 'piercing phrases'--'maugre my speeche's might'-- his reader may umbue them with her own (and different) sense, with her own 'lively forme,' as the reader becomes writer again creating an effect entirely the opposite of the one the original writer intended. The underlying implication is that words themselves are empty: they may, in short, say anything and nothing. As Richard Young notes, Stella 'transforms his poetry' and 'turns his own terms against him.' Here, in a way, we see Astrophil's frustration as he confronts a reader who uses 'the narration but as an imaginative ground-plot of a profitable invention' to produce her own meaning, rather than learning 'aright' the why and how of the maker. As A.C. Hamilton comments, 'In his opening program, [Astrophil] had assumed that Stella would be an ideal reader . . . . Unfortunately, she is not properly programmed.'[15]

Thus, although Waller is, I think, correct to suggest that *Astrophil and Stella* emphasizes 'the inventive role of the . . . reader who becomes . . . a producer of the work's meaning,' it is also important to realize that Sidney is ambivalent about this role and concerned about the challenge it potentially holds for the efficacy of the poet's work. And although Krieger is correct to suggest that Sidney confronts the emptiness of words, it is also important to realize that the invocation of Stella's presence and powers of transformation may resolve one part of the problem, but it raises another and equally crucial one. This may be why, in Sonnet 34, Sidney has Astrophil discuss with himself the motive for writing, and to consider the possibility that it remain a totally private activity, enacted for, by, and about the writer alone:

> Come let me write, 'And to what end?' To ease
>   A burthned hart. 'How can words ease, which are
> The glasses of thy dayly vexing care?'

Oft cruell fights well pictured forth do please.

Although the two voices of Astrophil are engaged in debate here, they share two common assumptions. The first is that words can and do represent and even embody his personal truth, and the second is that a writer's primary, if not only, audience is himself: Astrophil writes to ease his heart by expressing and therefore in a way releasing its burdens in words, and his words are mirrors of his feelings. Yet the allusion in the fourth line to the Aristotelian theory of imitation, while it also assumes the accuracy of representation, implicitly introduces a new dimension to the discussion. Astrophil's comment here seems still to concern his endeavor to ease and please himself through the accurate portrayal or picturing forth of his 'care,' but Aristotle's remark, and Sidney's reference to it in the *Apology*, concerns the effect of poetic imitation on other readers (Sidney uses Aristotle's remark as part of his argument for the superiority of the poet's power to 'move'). I am referring to his comment that 'Aristotle saith, those things which in themselves are horrible, as cruel battles, unnatural monsters, are made in poetical imitation delightful' (92.25-27). This leads into the second quatrain of the sonnet, where the question of the larger audience is explicitly addressed:

'Art not asham'd to publish thy disease?'
Nay, that may breed my fame, it is so rare:
'But will not wise men thinke thy words fonde ware?'
Then be they close, and so none shall displease.

Astrophil cannot maintain his limited concentration on himself as his only audience; despite his opening insistence that he writes for himself, he is compelled to consider his poetry's effect on others. When the troubling second voice raises the possibility that those words that picture forth so 'well' the burdens of his heart will be construed as foolish commodities, trifles--in other words, when the possibility of an unsympathetic audience is introduced--Astrophil tries again to restrict his audience and insist that the words should remain private: 'Then be they close.' The completion of that phrase, however--'and so none shall displease'--and its association with the earlier claim that 'Oft cruell fights well pictured forth do please'--sum up the problem: the only way that words can be made to retain their representative value and their original function (to ease) is to keep them private--if published, they may not only be construed 'fond ware,' but may also have an undesirable effect: they may 'displease.' But, Astrophil asks himself, is it worthwhile to write without a larger audience? The question appears to be a rhetorical one, and Astrophil simply juxtaposes to it another apparently rhetorical question: is it possible to feel and not to

The Limits of Language

write?:

> 'What idler thing, then speake and not be hard?'
> What harder thing then smart, and not to speake?

Astrophil must ultimately let go of the idea that he will write private poetry, yet he also acknowledges that it is as idle or vain or futile to speak and not be heard as it is to assume a compassionate reading from another.[16] It is impossible for Astrophil to reject or dismiss his readers, but once he acknowledges their presence, his entire analysis of why he writes and whether he should breaks down: 'Peace, foolish wit, with wit my wit is mard.' And he can only conclude with the basic dilemma, the source of which, as he reveals in his final phrase, is the power of that one special reader who constantly confutes his endeavor:

> Thus write I while I doubt to write, and wreake
> My harmes on Ink's poore losse, perhaps some find
> *Stella's* great powrs, that so confuse my mind.

Astrophil and Stella, then, like the *Apology*, does not resolve the issue of what words may say and not say. However, it does, occasionally, exploit the problem. Employing the characteristic wit, ingenuity and playfulness with which Sidney endows his poet/lover, Astrophil capitalizes on his predicament with language and audience, and turns the tables on Stella. In Sonnet 63, 'O Grammer rules,' Astrophil becomes the reader of Stella's words, not one who laments *her* transformation of *his* words, but one who himself transforms hers. Having 'crav'd the thing which ever she denies,' Astrophil reports Stella's response:

> She lightning *Love*, displaying *Venus'* skies,
> Least once should not be heard, twise said, No, No.

Then, showing how well he has learned the powers of readers from Stella herself, he proceeds to claim his victory. Despite--or rather because of--her attempt to be forceful and explicit in her expression of rejection, he manages to transform her denial into his triumph:

> For Grammer sayes (o this deare *Stella* weighe,)
> For Grammer sayes (to Grammer who sayes nay)
> That in one speech two Negatives affirme.

As Young comments, Astrophil here argues that 'the capricious tyranny over words' that Stella has exhibited is 'available to lovers as well as ladies.'[17] As sophistically as Sidney in the *Apology* converts Plato's attack on poets into praise of them, Astrophil uses Stella's narration as a ground-plot for his own profitable invention, willfully refusing to 'learn aright' the why and how of its maker. Sonnet 68 also shows Astrophil's own refusal to be an ideal reader, his insistence that he will be as perverse an audience as Stella has been. He begins with some truths that speak very much like flattery: Stella is the 'onely Planet of my light,' 'Light of my life, and life of my desire,' 'World of my wealth,' among other things. But in the second quatrain he wonders why Stella uses the persuasive power of her 'voice' to attempt to stifle his love:

> Why doest thou spend the treasures of thy sprite,
>   With voice more fit to wed *Amphion's* lyre,
>   Seeking to quench in me the noble fire,
> Fed by thy worth, and kindled by thy sight?

It is a futile attempt, he claims, for he will resist her 'sweet' breath and her 'choisest words':

> And all in vaine, for while thy breath most sweet,
> With choisest words, thy words with reasons rare,
> Thy reasons firmly set on *Vertue's* feet,
> Labour to kill in me this killing care:
>   O thinke I then, what paradise of joy
>   It is, so faire a Vertue to enjoy.

The almost prurient impact of the last line tells us that Astrophil will not only be able to withstand her verbal remonstrations to 'quench' his 'fire,' but also that he can and will subvert her intentions by changing the import of her words: while she tries to instill in him a virtue that will subdue his desire, he will be inspired to imagine and desire the enjoyment of her 'vertue'--i.e., her possession of Stella who is, as he claimed at the outset, 'life of my desire.'[18]

Just as Sidney, in Sonnet 34, had Astrophil analyze the motives for writing, he also has him analyze the motives for (mis)interpretation. In Sonnet 66, Astrophil describes a glimpse he had of Stella's face as she looked at him, and her blush upon discovering that he has been watching seems to him a possible indication of love. In Sonnet 67, he examines his reading of this. Although he is speaking here not of her words, but of her countenance, the language he uses to describe it--her 'eye's speech,' 'faire text,' 'margine'--suggests that his comments are relevant to the issues we have been discussing. He begins by questioning the reliability of his reading, and the personal motives that elicited it:

> Hope, art thou true, or doest thou flatter me?
>   Doth *Stella* now begin with piteous eye,
>   The ruines of her conquest to espie:
> Will she take time, before all wracked be?

> Her eye's-speech is translated thus by thee:
> But failst thou not in phrase so heavenly hie?

Just as he pondered, from the perspective of the writer, the efficacy of words that make truth speak like flattery, he now ponders, from the perspective of audience, whether interpretations blur these distinctions as well. First he requests a closer examination, in order to discover the truth:

> Looke on again, the faire text better trie:
> What blushing notes doest thou in margine see?
> What sighes stolne out, or kild before full borne?
> Hast thou found such and such like arguments?
> Or art thou else to comfort me forsworne?

But although he distrusts the legitimacy of his hope's translation of Stella's 'eye's-speech' and desires a second look at the 'text,' he ultimately chooses to forgo the problem, the attempt to 'learn aright':

> Well, how so thou interpret the contents,
> I am resolv'd thy errour to maintaine,
> Rather then by more truth to get more paine.

Astrophil decides he would rather rest with an interpretation that expresses his own desires than risk learning a truth of Stella's that may cause him discomfort.

Sidney rounds out his insight into the writer's dilemma through this insight into the way the audience responds. Be it Astrophil and his words that well set forth his mind, or Stella and the attempted clarity of her 'No, No,' the speaker cannot control his or her language and its effect on readers, who will construe it according to their own natures and predilections. If words must speak like flattery, it is because we cannot fix specific meanings to words and because readers often desire a kind of self-flattery more than truth, (re)-making the text into an image of their own minds. Hence Astrophil and Stella are ultimately condemned--despite their momentary and conditional reconciliation--to remain at a stand-still at the end of the sequence: he cannot move Stella as he would like (and obtain 'grace) and she cannot move him (and quench his desire). Sidney manages to figure forth his own unresolved uneasiness about the complicated relations between readers and writers--the way they can use and abuse each other, and the challenge to the efficacy of words this demonstrates--as Astrophil and Stella alternate roles as writers and readers of their own and each other's texts.

NOTES

1. Murray Krieger, 'Poetic Presence and Illusion I: Renaissance Theory and the Duplicity of Metaphor,' in *Poetic*

Presence and Illusion. Essays in Critical History and Theory (Baltimore, 1979), pp. 25, 26, 12.

2. Krieger, pp. 15-17. Krieger makes these comments specifically in relation to Sonnet 35. See Miller, '"Love doth hold my hand': Writing and Wooing in the Sonnets of Sidney and Spenser,' *ELH*, 46 (1979), pp. 541-58. Although we are dealing with different issues for Renaissance poets, Krieger and I make some similar general points about the importance of Stella's presentation to Sidney's aesthetic; however, we offer different perspectives when we discuss the poet's ultimate attitude towards her role and his motive for invoking it. See Richard Young's comments on Stella's 'metamorphic power' in 'English Petrarke: A Study of Sidney's *Astrophil and Stella*," in *Three Studies in the Renaissance: Sidney, Jonson, Milton, Yale Studies in English*, Vol. 138 (New Haven, 1958), pp. 55 ff. Compare Krieger's analysis of this sonnet, p. 15.

3. The source of Krieger's and my different readings may be that Krieger emphasizes Stella as the 'only object of representation, or presentation' in the sonnets (p. 13), whereas I see Astrophil trying to 'represent' himself as well. Krieger bases his premise on a reading of the last line of Sonnet 1--'"Foole," said my Muse to me, "looke in thy heart and write."' Krieger comments, 'This is not just an easy call for a lover's direct emotional sincerity. More than this, the poet . . . is assuming our awareness of an elaborate Petrarchan conceit: the lover installs in his heart the image of his beloved who lodges there substantially' (p. 13). Krieger is right to remind us of the convention behind the Muse's instruction; but as Hamilton (*Sidney*, pp. 193-94, n. 39) and Rudenstine (*Sidney's Poetic Development*, pp. 200-01) suggest, both readings are equally available and equally important. As Rudenstine explains, Astrophil is urged both 'to focus upon Stella' *and* 'not to neglect the passions of his own heart . . . Such an interpretation need not give way to more broadly "romantic" readings of either the poem or the sequence. Astrophil's primary goal remains an objective one: not self-exploration and self-expression as ends in themselves, but the expression of personal feeling for the purposes of rhetorical persuasion' (p. 200). And Sonnet 1 as a whole reveals Astrophil's purpose--to communicate his feelings to Stella, that she might 'know' and 'pity' and ultimately yield. Once this is taken into account, we can see, I think, that the sort of 'transformation' by Stella that Krieger speaks of raises as many problems for Astrophil as it resolves.

4. Gary Waller, 'Acts of Reading: The Production of Meaning in *Astrophil and Stella*,' *SLitI*, 15, No. 1 (1982), pp. 30, 23, 25, 27, 31. See Hallett Smith's interesting comments on the 'double audience' of *Astrophil and Stella* in *Elizabethan Poetry*, pp. 145-48. Waller implies that even in the sonnets where Astrophil claims to write only for Stella,

the poems primarily address the larger audience (see his analysis of Sonnet 54, p. 31).

5. Rudenstine, p. 152.

6. Smith, p. 148.

7. Margaret Ferguson, 'Sidney's *A Defence of Poetry*: A Retrial,' *Boundary 2*, 7 (1979), pp. 75, 79. My discussion here of Sidney's attitude towards readers in the *Apology* is indebted to Ferguson's excellent study. Waller notes that Sidney in the *Apology* 'wrestles with the inherited, residual model of the reader's passivity,' but defines his goal as 'to make the reader no longer merely "a consumer, but a producer of the text."' Waller sees the *Apology* as 'grasping towards such issues,' and *Astrophil and Stella* as making 'much more obviously open-ended demands of its readers' (p. 30). My point is that Sidney's ambivalence about this is clearly depicted in the *Apology* and similarly expressed in the sonnets.

8. A. Leigh DeNeef, 'Rereading Sidney's *Apology*,' *JMRS*, 10 (1980), p. 179. See also pp. 168-9, 186-7, and Ferguson, especially pp. 70-71, 80.

9. Ronald Levao, 'Sidney's Feigned *Apology*,' *PMLA*, 94 (1979), p. 227. See also John M. Wallace, '"Examples Are Best Precepts": Readers and Meaning in Seventeenth-Century Poetry,' *Critical Inquiry*, 1 (1974), pp. 281-82. For a counter-argument, see DeNeef, pp. 178-79.

10. Ferguson aptly characterizes Sidney's ambivalence about the roles and powers of readers and writers in her conclusion that the *Apology* ultimately 'offers a model of the relation between text and reader which consists of a constant turning of master into servant and servant into master' (p. 85). My discussion of this phrase from the *Apology*--which Ferguson only briefly and without analysis refers to in passing (and she only refers to the second half of the phrase)-- lends further support to her conclusion.

11. Thomas Wilson, *The Arte of Rhetorique*, in *English Literary Criticism: The Renaissance*, ed. O.B. Hardison, Jr. (Englewood Cliffs, N.J., 1963), p. 27; Puttenham, *The Arte of English Poesy*, Book III, Chp. 2 (Kent, Ohio, 1970; facsimile reproduction of 1906 report by A. Constable & Co.), p. 154. I have modernized the *u/v* and *f/s* spelling.

12. Ringler notes the allusion to the emblem of Hercules in his edition (p. 477). On the alliance between oratory and poetry in the Renaissance, see Sidney's own statement in the *Apology* that they 'both have such an affinity in this wordish consideration' (p. 139); and the comments by Ferguson, pp. 63-64, and O.B. Hardison, 'The Orator and the Poet: The Dilemma of Humanist Literature,' *JMRS*, 1 (1971), pp. 33-44. Hardison also makes some interesting observations about the emblem of Hercules in his article.

13. See, for example, Ringler, p. 477; and David Kalstone, ed. *The Selected Poetry and Prose of Sidney* (New York, 1970), p. 152.

14. Shepherd, in his 'Introduction' to his edition of the *Apology* (1965), pp. 60, 226. Shepherd's insightful comments on this sonnet (pp. 55-61) are relevant to my discussion here. See also James Finn Cotter, 'The Songs in *Astrophil and Stella*,' *SP*, 67 (1970), pp. 178-200, who discusses the classical five-part division of rhetoric and explains that 'pronunciation, the last step in the rhetorical-poetic process of creation, becomes the first in the transmission of the idea' (p. 184).

15. Young, p. 60; A.C. Hamilton, 'Sidney's *Astrophel and Stella* as a Sonnet Sequence,' *ELH*, 36 (1969), p. 82.

16. Cf. Hamilton's comments on this poem and its relation to Donne's 'The Triple Fool' in *Sidney*, pp. 95-96 and 196-97, n. 66; and in 'Sidney's *Astrophel and Stella* . . .' p. 76.

17. Young, p. 61.

18. See Young's comments on the ambiguity of the word 'virtue' in this sonnet (p. 36).

SIDNEY'S PRESENCE IN LYRIC VERSE OF THE LATER ENGLISH RENAISSANCE

Jon A. Quitslund

I will begin with a few general remarks which will provide an arena of hypotheses within which I can examine a group of short poems composed between 1580 and 1630. First, I take the concepts of 'mannerism' and 'anti-mannerism' from historians of art and others who have attempted to describe the period style of the later Renaissance. The period initiated in England by Sidney was characterized by restless experimentation in search of both stylistic norms and stylistic individuality. Sidney looked back to Petrarch, and he regarded Petrarchism critically. In Petrarch, and again in Sannazaro, to name only two important predecessors, he found examples of involuted style expressive of involuted consciousness. Like them he was aware of classical norms and forms, but he was moved most often to articulate non-classical, *extra*ordinary states of mind--a mannerist's experience of 'difficulty' and 'the marvelous.' None of this was consistent with servile or superficial imitation. Sidney's genius combined two contrary abilities which the poets following him would have to find within themselves: a capacity to assimilate conventions in style and subject matter, and a detached attitude toward conventions, by turns rebellious and playful, expressed in a highly individual voice. Also, the evolution of taste after Sidney's death encouraged some poets to reject his *maniera* in favor of anti-mannerist or neo-classical norms.

Second, I take from historians who have studied Sidney's reputation the recognition that few lyric poets in the fifty-year period I have defined wrote without respect for Sidney's verse--or indeed, without imitating or otherwise echoing it. The range of Sidney's influence includes many who could be seen as *reacting against* the Petrarchan mode. I have chosen for discussion in this paper a number of poems fundamentally different from Sidney's own, in which an assertion of difference is as important as any echoing of a model among Sidney's poems. I believe that influence, in Sidney's period, rarely works inadvertently, and it is most interesting when it cannot be described as 'borrowing' or 'echoing.' It may entail the reinvention of a predecessor's scenario, and a radically different entrance and exit. The audience may hear in this and what follows some borrowing on my part from Harold Bloom, and I will invite comparison of my style and convention to his. Bloom has been anxious to show that the ways a poet is influenced by a predecessor are deep, devious, and at the heart of the creative process; I am concerned here not to penetrate to depths unplumbed by Bloom, but perhaps to roll back the date by which an anxious experience of influence may be seen to have begun.

Bloom observes with his characteristic panache that 'the poet of any guilt culture whatsoever cannot initiate himself into a fresh chaos; he is compelled to accept a lack of priority in creation.'[1] Beginning with Sidney and giving more attention to several of his successors, I would like to interpret some of the consequences of that lack of priority which--and I agree with Bloom--must condition even a writer such as Sidney who is hailed as a bearer of new light in a dark time. The 'scene of writing' for Sidney, and again for his successors, is Astrophil's situation in his first sonnet: the 'fresh chaos' of a personal 'woe' is mediated by 'inventions fine,' and even when the poet turns from 'others' leaves' and 'others' feet' to his own heart, he sees only the imagery and emotions which centuries of literary culture have put there.

Sidney was, I believe, relatively untroubled by his lack of priority. He came upon a scene whose drabness he could, with some justification, lament, while at the same time he made his poetry within the structural and thematic boundaries of the mid-Tudor poets, as Germaine Warkentin shows in her essay in this collection. The situation for those contemporaries who survived him, and for the next generation or two, was quite different. For the lyric poets among them it was Sidney, more than any other English poet, who determined their 'lack of priority,' and they were obliged to turn that situation into an advantage if they could. They could do so more readily than the guilt-ridden poets of Bloom's romantic mythology, partly because Renaissance culture had tamed the mysteries and terrors of influence by the rituals of imitation, and partly because of the nature of Sidney's legacy.

I have come to the third of my hypotheses or generalizations. Although Sidney alive was, by all accounts, an enormously invigorating presence on the scene of literature and learning, his greatest gift to his fellow poets was, quite literally, a legacy: the availability, with no strings attached, of the poetry that survived his early death. The exemplary Sir Philip Sidney might have been expected to rule, as he saw fit, the monarchy of English letters, and to do so for many years, but he died with much of his own promise unfulfilled, as Professor van Dorsten has emphasized. His death was one of many in the 1580s which provoked the muses to tears over an apparently stalled movement to renew Christian faith and humane culture in England. I suggest, however, that Sidney's tragic death served ultimately to liberate energies and encourage emulation. Spenser mourns Sidney in *Astrophel* as a pathetic Adonis figure; I suggest that in Spenser's poetry and in that of a host of other poets, Sidney was, like Adonis, 'by succession made perpetual' (*F.Q.* III vi 47.6).

Sidney's life and death recommended veneration but did not inspire awe; the mixture of sophistication and immaturity in his poetry made it both imitable and a perfect foil for further innovation. Sidney's career was full of potentiality and marked by incompleteness, hence much of his importance to other poets. It has been observed that, had Shakespeare died at Sidney's age, we would have no notion of his greatness, the implication being that Sidney, like Keats, probably died with his greatest poetry unwritten. But that potential greatness might, in its realization, have had a chilling effect on other men's creativity. I have heard it suggested that, had he lived into the 1590s, Sidney would have been the arbiter of a strict Protestant classicism such as his sister Mary espoused, and that he might thereby have discouraged or misdirected such authors as Marlowe, Nashe, Greene, Spenser, Shakespeare, and Donne; Chapman and Jonson would have been obliged to stand in his shade. It is plausible, I believe, that the influence of the deceased Sidney, in people's memories and their libraries, greatly exceeded what he could have achieved in the flesh. 'The death of the poet was kept from his poems,' and 'he became his admirers'; perhaps these things can be said more appropriately of Sidney than of Yeats. We know how fertile memory was for Petrarch, and Petrarch created a reputation for himself--not to mention what he did for Laura--much larger than his life. After Laura, think also of poor Penelope, obliged to live out a rather sordid actual life after being immortalized in verse. But I digress. By dying and leaving a poetic legacy, first treasured in manuscripts and then spread abroad in several printed editions, Sidney became the cause that wit was in other men; he enabled poets with various gifts in several phases of the English Renaissance each to be true to him and at the same time to establish their individuality.

Sidney's friends, disciples, and later successors in poetry, courtliness, and Protestantism found several excellences in him, and his early death freed them to make what they liked of him, as a prototype either for imitation or for correction. Death, we might say without irreverence, bestowed a Sidney upon the world to make many Sidneys. There was Sidney 'the pattern of chivalry,' a pattern he became 'only by dying,' as Ronald Rebholz has pointed out;[2] alive he had been admired but also disadvantaged, frustrated, a peripheral figure. In Sidney the writer--and here, again, I am focusing upon the lyric verse--his fellow poets found a master of intricate forms, complex syntax, harmonious diction, and a rich figurative language. This eloquent and artificial Sidney alternates in *Astrophil and Stella* with a colloquial poet, a ventriloquist, a manipulator of speech rhythms and the emotions of dramatic moments. One voice of the ventriloquist is that of the plain speaker, a man committed to sincerity, to putting the simple into the complex. Renaissance poets also found in Sidney (not that they would describe him in our terms) an ironist and an analyst of subjective states, enmeshed in the contradictions of courtliness, playing ruefully or irreverently with the uncertainties of a divided consciousness. Sidney the moralist--Stoic and Calvinist by turns--is complicated by Sidney the aesthete and the melancholic. Since Sidney himself consistently questioned the value of models and received opinions, it is natural to find his successors alluding to him only to go their own way, but his work is so full of different possibilities that to reject one is often a pretext for silently choosing another of the paths down which Sidney himself travelled.

Gary Waller has found in *Astrophil and Stella* 'an exemplary embodiment of potential rather than realized and closed meanings.'[3] Something of this was recognized, though not in so many words, in Sidney's own time. Waller and others in this collection discuss the dynamics of the reader's role in response to Sidney's poetry. Focusing on the several things that other Renaissance poets did with Sidney's style and themes, I will present those followers as readers in their writing, engaged both in imitation of their chief precursor and in finding words for the independent authenticity which Sidney's precepts and example required.

I will begin with Fulke Greville, in whose poetry I see almost the full gamut of responses to Sidney that can be noted in the work of other poets. Greville felt the tragedy of Sidney's death most as a limiting of possibilities, and yet it also served to remove from life to art an influence toward which he was at best ambivalent. Greville in the earlier poems of *Caelica* is either mid-Tudor and pre-Sidneian, or an awkward imitator of his *alter ego* (an example of this kind of imitation is seen in *Caelica* 35). In his mature verse, on the other hand, Greville speaks with seriousness, directness, and hard-won wisdom which Sidney surely would have admired, but which find few parallels in his own poetry. Greville's anxious attentiveness to Sidney's memory makes him seem at times the very pattern of Harold Bloom's *bête noir*, the 'weak' poet, but he can also command a strength that shows where Sidney was weak--or where, perhaps, we had better put aside Bloom's vocabulary in favor of a different account of the dynamics of influence, imitation and innovation.

Greville's *Life of Sidney* presents the man and the poet as a paragon deserving imitation, yet to imitate is to accept a dependent role in which Greville the poet is uncomfortable.

'Many gentlemen excellently learned among us will not deny but
that they affected to row and steer their course in his wake.'
Here Sidney is seen, not without envy, the courtier's vice,
as out front and in the larger vessel, moved by the wind
rather than the labor of oarsmen. There is a different ambivalence in Greville's admiration for the *Arcadia*. Sidney's
'Arcadian antiques' (surely a pun) are acceptable with the
proviso 'that his end in them was not vanishing pleasures
alone,' and he adds, 'yet I do wish that work may be the last
in this kind.' He has already complained of 'the strangeness
or perplexedness of witty fictions, in which the affections,
or imagination, may perchance find exercise and entertainment
but the memory and judgement no enriching at all.' Such an
austere taste, impatient with 'delicate images,' had been dominant in England before Sidney, and here it is again in a
memoir of Jacobean disillusionment. In Greville's account,
Sidney begins to seem a splendid sport of nature. Sidney
would not, I think, have made Greville's distinction between
'the images of wit' and 'the images of life'; he would not
have admitted to a 'creeping genius,' which in his terms would
have been 'captived to the truth of a foolish world.' For
Greville, however, such a voice is the appropriate means of
addressing 'those only that are weather-beaten in the sea of
this world, . . . having lost the sight of their gardens and
groves.'[4] As time wore on beyond the idealistic years that
formed Sidney's thought, there were many such readers.

Greville's strengths are best compared to Sidney's in
Astrophil and Stella 99 and *Caelica* 100 (number 99 in the
Warwick MS.).[5]

> When far spent night perswades each mortall eye,
>   To whom nor art nor nature graunteth light,
>   To lay his then marke wanting shafts of sight,
> Clos'd with their quivers in sleep's armory;
> With windowes ope then most my mind doth lie,
>   Viewing the shape of darknesse and delight,
>   Takes in that sad hue, which with th'inward night
> Of his mazde powers keepes perfit harmony:
>   But when birds charme, and that sweete aire, which is
> Morne's messenger, with rose enameld skies
> Cals each wight to salute the floure of blisse;
>   In tombe of lids then buried are mine eyes,
>   Forst by their Lord, who is asham'd to find
>   Such light in sense, with such a darkned mind.
>
> In night when colours all to black are cast,
> Distinction lost, or gone down with the light,
> The eye, a watch to inward senses placed,
> Not seeing, yet still having power of sight,
> Gives vain alarums to the inward sense,
> Where fear, stirred up with witty tyranny,

> Confounds all powers, and thorough self-offense,
> Doth forge and raise impossibility:
> Such as in thick depriving darknesses
> Proper reflections of the error be,
> And images of self-confusednesses
> Which hurt imaginations only see;
> > And from this nothing seen, tells news of devils,
> > Which but expressions be of inward evils.

Greville has managed in his sonnet to match Sidney's skill with a syntax woven to fit the sonnet's frame; it is something he seldom even attempts. Clearly Greville was writing with Sidney's poem in mind: we find in both sonnets not only the nocturnal scene, but reflections on vision and introspection. What is most noteworthy, of course, is Greville's reorientation of an introspective consciousness. Sidney's poem is a study of a lover's melancholy, in which the lover is at odds with the order of nature, exquisitely aware of the fact, and powerless to change it. In Greville's sonnet a similar melancholy 'sits on brood,' but with a different subject matter, religious rather than erotic. His is precisely the sophisticated consciousness that troubled Hamlet. What is for Sidney a defect of the will which has 'mazde' the mind has been relocated in the misinformed 'inward senses' (the *sensus communis* and imagination, confused by the passion of fear, not love). The drama of a lover's temporary predicament has been developed into a trenchant analysis of what Richard Waswo calls 'projection.'[6] Several things are lost--or should we say set aside--as a result of Greville's reorientation of the theme: the poetry is no longer character-centered and devoted to registering individual perceptions; it seeks generality rather than lyric grace, and chooses an old-fashioned allegorical schema as the vehicle of a discursive theme. Both poems employ allegorical conceits in which the eye is a servant of the mind in his tower (in Sidney's poem a bowman who retires for the night, and in Greville's an overzealous night-watchman). The personifications are more numerous and abstract in Greville's sonnet. Something like Sidney's luxuriant metaphors remain, but the tone is deliberately flat. Greville also omits all reference to the relief found in Sidney's first tercet: the external realities of a beautiful morning.

Next, I wish to consider a few of Shakespeare's sonnets. A glance at his Sonnet 24 will show something of the strangeness of Sidney's presence in this most puzzling of sequences.

> Mine eye hath played the painter and hath stelled,
> Thy beauty's form in table of my heart,
> My body is the frame wherein 'tis held,
> And perspective it is best painter's art.
> For through the painter must you see his skill,

> To find where your true image pictured lies,
> Which in my bosom's shop is hanging still,
> That hath his windows glazéd with thine eyes:
> Now see what good turns eyes for eyes have done,
> Mine eyes have drawn thy shape, and thine for me
> Are windows to my breast, where-through the sun
> Delights to peep, to gaze therein on thee;
>   Yet eyes this cunning want to grace their art,
>   They draw but what they see, know not the heart.[7]

This poem seems to me a deliberate parody of Sidney's manner; the first rhyme-word, 'stelled,' may be meant as a wink or twinkle that gives the game away. The conceit is not one that Sidney uses--Astrophil's famous heart contains a verbal rather than a painted image--, and the infrequent references to painting in *Astrophil and Stella* (in Sonnets 1, 2, 7, and 45) suggest that for Sidney the 'best painter's art' would be *chiaroscuro*, not a tricky use of perspective. But the conceit developed so laboriously in Shakespeare's sonnet is the kind of thing that Sidney managed with great skill. Shakespeare builds up ingenious conceits often enough, but the best of them are quite unlike Sidney's in structure and effect. Sometimes technique triumphs over triviality in Sidney's sonnets, and that somewhat immature artificiality seems to have given rise to awkward imitation or parody as well as successful emulation. I suggest that what we have here, parody or not, is a genuine instance of 'poetic misprision.' A patient reader who reaches the couplet will notice, however, that its wry twist is the most genuinely Sidneian part of the poem, and also the most characteristic of Shakespeare. The uneasy last line, 'They draw but what they see, know not the heart,' voices an insecurity absent from *Astrophil and Stella* and pervasive in Shakespeare's sequence. Assimilation of a predecessor's lessons gave Shakespeare his own voice.

    Sonnet 84 offers a straightforward instance of indebtedness acknowledged by allusion.

> Who is it that says most, which can say more,
> Than this rich praise, that you alone, are you?
> In whose confine immuréd is the store,
> Which should example where your equal grew.
> Lean penury within that pen doth dwell,
> That to his subject lends not some small glory,
> But he that writes of you, if he can tell,
> That you are you, so dignifies his story.
> Let him but copy what in you is writ,
> Not making worse what nature made so clear,
> And such a counterpart shall fame his wit,
> Making his style admiréd every where.
>   You to your beauteous blessings add a curse,
>   Being fond on praise, which makes your praises worse.

Writing of the difficulty of praising his unique subject effectively, Shakespeare has made rather witty use of two Sidney sonnets (3 and 35) in which Sidney considers the same problem. A reader coming fresh from *Astrophil and Stella* will notice that there is something funny going on in the opening lines of both this and the next sonnet in Shakespeare's sequence. 'Who is it that says most, which can say more,/Than this *rich* praise, that you alone, are you?' the poet asks (emphasis added). And in Sonnet 85, 'My tongue-tied muse in manners holds her still,/While comments of your praise *rich*ly compiled' are offered by the rival poet in 'previous phrase by all the Muses filed.' Engaged in justifying his own plain sincerity and reticence against the claims of the rival's flattery, Shakespeare has turned to his own use the word 'rich,' so notably used by Sidney in Sonnets 35, 37, and elsewhere. Perhaps one good pun begets another. It is singularly appropriate that Shakespeare's literary rivalry should include an in-group joke. In lines 10 and 11 of *Astrophil and Stella* Sonnet 35 we find, 'and now long needy Fame/Both even grow rich, naming my Stella's name.' Offering 'this rich praise, that you alone, are you,' in place of the rival's 'previous phrase,' Shakespeare is himself concerned to be literary, but with tongue in cheek rather than ostentatious artifice.

He makes Astrophil's difficulties and professions of sincerity his own. Borrowing his poetic strategy from another poet's praise, he risks negating his claim 'that you alone, are you.' In lines 7 and 8 of Sonnet 84 Shakespeare claims, 'But he that writes of you, if he can tell,/That you are you, so dignifies his story,' and he goes on to observe that such a simple, faithful story 'shall fame his wit,/Making his style admirèd every where.' A similar message is found in the last three lines of *Astrophil and Stella* 35, 'Wit learne in thee perfection to expresse,/Not thou by praise, but praise in thee is raisde:/It is a praise to praise, when thou art praisde.' These resemblances are thematic, not verbal, but Shakespeare has worked into lines 9 and 10 of Sonnet 84 an emphatic allusion to the ending of Astrophil's third sonnet, which dismisses a host of rival poets: 'all my deed/But Copying is, what in her Nature writes.' Sidney was not, of course, the first to base a profession of sincerity upon rejection of art and an almost wordless copying of Nature's work, so we should not be surprised to find Shakespeare following him so closely. The echoes I have noted do not, I think, add irony to his praise; they only reveal him being playfully serious at the expense of the rival poet. And they illuminate for us, I believe, the nature of a literary tradition and Sidney's position in it. Imitation of one kind--recreative--should be distinguished from the flattering pastichery of the 'dainty-wits' around Astrophil and the 'well refinèd pen' of Shakespeare's rival.

In Sonnet 84 it is important to Shakespeare to resemble

Sidney in praising a beloved who is, like Stella, something of a paragon. The effect is to stress the continuity of Shakespeare's experience and poetic intent with Sidney's. The echoes of *Astrophil and Stella* 7, 'When Nature made her chief work, Stella's eyes,' which figure in Shakespeare's Sonnet 127 have quite a different effect. In Shakespeare's poem, 'In the old age black was not counted fair,' which inaugurates the group dominated by the Dark Lady, Sidney's hyperbolic praise suddenly seems to belong to 'the old age,' when love had a different object and poetry arose from different impulses. But when I remark on the difference between these two poems, my point is not that Shakespeare's subverts or rejects Sidney's. Sonnet 127 gains resonance from Sidney's, even more than Greville's poem had from *Astrophil and Stella* 99; Shakespeare is drawn nostalgically to 'the old age,' which he had celebrated in Sonnet 68 (thematically the opposite number to 127), and echoes of Sidney are consistent with that nostalgia. But in both Sonnets 68 and 127 Shakespeare protests the ascendancy of art over nature, and this attitude creates a contrast to the patently artificial procedures by which nature's 'chiefe worke, *Stella's* eyes,' are enhanced for us in Sonnet 7 and many others like it. Sidney's theme, the lady's eyes, and his techniques for developing it belong squarely in the Petrarchan tradition, despite the fact that Stella's eyes are unconventionally black. With Shakespeare, on the other hand, the extent to which his conceit resembles Sidney's only calls attention to his radical difference, heard in the protest at the heart of the poem, 'Sweet beauty hath no name no holy bower,/But is profaned, if not lives in disgrace.'

    The differences between the two poems are most clearly seen where they are most alike, in the sestet, when they associate black with mourning. In Sidney's sonnet it is Love, not Stella, who mourns, 'To honour all their deaths, who for her bleed.' Stella herself is aloof from both suffering and sorrow. Shakespeare, on the other hand, has no need for the god of love. His mistress' eyes 'seem' to mourn the prevalence of artificial beauties. They mourn so attractively (so artfully, perhaps) 'that every tongue says beauty should look so,' and men turn away from those whose artifice slanders creation, but also from 'Sweet beauty,' the genuine article, which continues to live in disgrace. The bleeding of Stella's many conquests, which of course is more amusing than pathetic as long as we keep our distance from Astrophil, has been stanched: in Shakespeare's sonnet the love of black beauty is a cooler business. It may also be a more serious error. Stella was nothing but admirable, at least in Astrophil's eyes. As nature's 'chief work,' Stella's eyes offer evidence of both nature's exemplary artistry and her commitment to an artist's proper purpose, which is well-tempered 'delight' rather than the dazzling of susceptible men. Astrophil also finds evidence that nature can work miracles with a grace beyond the reach of art. Shakespeare's mistress inhabits an entirely different world. She isn't seen as nature's work of art, because art is in essence counterfeiting; she is only a woman who agrees with the poet in mourning the general decay of values and the passing of 'the old age,' and Shakespeare wishes to believe that her sadness is sincere, not artful. But since nature is decadent and art is false, any purpose (and purpose is suggested by 'Therefore' in line 9 and 'Yet so . . ./That . . .' in the couplet) the Dark Lady's mourning may serve is suspect.

Shakespeare's sonnets prepare us for John Donne, whose lyrics exhibit further developments away from Sidney's handling of form, diction, and themes. Donne strikes out on his own in many respects, even more than Sidney had done, but one can sometimes observe his appreciation of Sidney as a major predecessor. Ben Jonson thought the relationship worthy of comment, and his advice to his own disciples assimilates both poets' work to a pattern of cultural history and a sequence of styles. I quote from *Timber:* 'And as it is fit to read the best Authors to youth first, so let them be of the openest, and clearest. As *Livy* before *Sallust*, *Sidney* before *Donne*.'[8] Perhaps Jonson's own urgent need to keep Donne at a distance speaks in this comment more than anything else, but it remains good advice, I think, and indicates a sense of history that Donne may have shared with Jonson.

There are a number of allusions to and transformations of Sidneian models among Donne's poems: the relationship of 'The Ecstasy' to the Eighth Song in *Astrophil and Stella* is perhaps the most familiar example. Donne's indebtedness is not expressed in such verbal echoes as we have seen in Shakespeare's sonnets, although a close study of patterns in Donne's syntax might show that he learned much of his manner from Sidney. A look at *Astrophil and Stella* 21 and 'The Canonization' will illuminate both common traits and differences.

> Your words my friend (right healthfull caustiks) blame
>   My young minde marde, whom *Love* doth windlas so,
>   That mine owne writings like bad servants show
> My wits, quicke in vaine thoughts, in vertue lame:
> That *Plato* I read for nought, but if he tame
>   Such coltish gyres, that to my birth I owe
>   Nobler desires, least else that friendly foe,
> Great expectation, weare a traine of shame.
> For since mad March great promise made of me,
> If now the May of my yeares much decline,
> What can be hoped my harvest time will be?
> Sure you say well, your wisdome's golden mine
>   Dig deepe with learning's spade, now tell me this,
>   Hath this world ought so faire as *Stella* is?

It is not too much, I think, to say that Sidney's impatience
and sarcasm in poems such as this made possible Donne's more
dramatic monologues. Donne pulls some of the same stops in
his tirade, and offers similar admissions that love is self-
destructive.[9]

> For God's sake hold your tongue, and let me love.
>   Or chide my palsy, or my gout,
> My five grey hairs, or ruined fortune flout,
>   With wealth your state, your mind with arts improve,
>   Take you a course, get you a place,
>   Observe his Honour, or his Grace,
> Or the King's real, or his stamped face
>   Contemplate; what you will, approve,
>   So you will let me love.
>   . . .
> Call us what you will, we are made such by love;
>   Call her one, me another fly,
> We are tapers too, and at our own cost die,
>   And we in us find the eagle and the dove;
>   The phoenix riddle hath more wit
>   By us; we two being one, are it.
> So to one neutral thing both sexes fit.
>   We die and rise the same, and prove
>   Mysterious by this love.

One difference between the poems, of course, is that
Astrophil's friend can appeal to 'Nobler desires' and 'Great
expectation,' while Donne reminds himself and his antagonist
of an already 'ruined fortune,' and he expends much energy
describing the goings on, the getting and spending, in a world
from which he has withdrawn. In the years separating Donne
from Sidney, the court and the lyric speaker have aged con-
siderably. Astrophil was susceptible to a sense of shame,
and 'this world' consisted for him largely of people who hoped
for his reformation. In 'The Canonization,' apart from one
intrusive moralist—more a visitor from Sidney's poem than a
real friend of Donne's—the world is supposed to be indiffer-
ent to the lover's life or death until, at the end of the
poem, Donne has argued that lovers left in the world should
invoke the transcendent pattern he and his beloved have formed. Sidney's poetry, in which the lover is seen enmeshed in
the fabric of courtly society and its moral values, is translated by Donne into the furniture of a private world, in which
the basis for human relationships—between lover and beloved,
between the poet and his audience of connoisseurs—can be redefined to the speaker's liking. Astrophil holds only one
trump card: 'Hath this world aught so fair as Stella is?'
Apart from this rhetorical question, which could be answered
by suspicion that beauty is but a snare, Astrophil can offer
only sarcastic submission to his friend's good judgment.

Donne, by contrast, has himself taken possession of 'wisdom's
golden mine,' and he digs deep for evidence that lovers 'die
and rise the same, and prove/Mysterious by this love.' Only
the smallest germs of this attitude toward love are present
in Sidney's poetry, and they are found in a matrix not favorable to development. Donne omitted from 'The Canonization'
and the other major poems in his *Songs and Sonets* none of
Astrophil's contradictory qualities: his speaker is self-
absorbed, hyperbolic, ingenious in argument, both idealistic
and unprincipled, and he is in one poem what Astrophil is in
many. Donne has also made his lover more of a wit and more
experienced in love and its lore than Astrophil; going still
further, he has emphasized and ironized his self-sufficiency
by detaching the speaker from both society and the moral
absolutes of Nature, Love, Beauty, Reason, and Virtue.

I will complete the pattern of this survey rather abruptly by a few references to George Herbert's 'Jordan' poems.
As the scion of a family proud of its connections with the
Sidneys, Herbert had even more reason than Ben Jonson to honor
Sir Philip and his poetry. Despite differences in subject
matter and form (differences that disappear if we include the
metrical Psalms in our thinking about Sidney), Herbert's poetry is, I would judge, indebted even more deeply and broadly
than Donne's to Sidney's example. I am thinking of Herbert's
refined colloquialism, his playfulness, the intertwining of
narrative and discourse, surprising twists in his trains of
thought, and carefully controlled ironies--self-directed
ironies rather than the counter-factual hyperboles of Donne.
Some of Herbert's urbanity was mediated through Jonson and
other poets with classical tastes, but it stemmed ultimately
from Sidney. I am suggesting that Herbert has much less in
common with Donne than the convenience of literary historians has always implied. There is no equivalent to Donne's
egocentric subjectivity in Herbert's poetry; his self-con-
sciousness is more like that of the poet who created Astrophil in order to achieve detachment from his aspirations and
his follies. This is evident in Herbert's variations on
Sidney's themes. The second 'Jordan' poem is patterned upon
the third sonnet of *Astrophil and Stella*, 'Let dainty wits
cry on the sisters nine,' taken together with the first sonnet. I will quote only Herbert's last stanza:[10]

>   As flames do work and wind, when they ascend,
>   So did I weave my self into the sense.
>   But while I bustled, I might hear a friend
>   Whisper, *How wide is all this long pretence!*
>   *There is in love a sweetness ready penned:*
>   *Copy out only that, and save expense.*

This recalls Sidney's lines, 'How then? Even thus: in Stella's
face I read/What love and beauty be; then all my deed/But

copying is, what in her nature writes.'

From Herbert's point of view, of course, Stella's face belongs in the category of 'fictions only and false hair' described in 'Jordan (I),' and her existence independent of Astrophil is illusory. In his own poetry, in turn, the 'sweetness ready penned' that exists 'in love' to be copied by the poet will be found only after he has said, 'So did I weave my self into the sense.' Love's sweetness is an aspect of the poet's life in Herbert, just as 'the blackest face of woe' is an aspect of Astrophil's. But it is also true that 'God is love,' and not the mischievous and make-believe love-god of Sidney's sonnets, either. Love, the God within, simple and paradoxical, is accessible to the simple copyist, not to the imitator of Sidney's 'dainty wits,' which Herbert earlier in 'Jordan (II)' felt obliged to be.

> When first my lines of heav'nly joys made mention,
> Such was their luster, they did so excel,
> That I sought out quaint words, and trim invention,
> My thoughts began to burnish, sprout, and swell,
> Curling with metaphors a plain intention,
> Decking the sense, as if it were to sell.

The simple conclusion of this poem is one that Sidney himself might have come to, given world enough and time: we often find him putting the simple into the complex. But since events were ordered differently, we can thank Sidney for having provided whispered inspiration for the words that many copyists penned in the later Renaissance.

NOTES

1. *The Anxiety of Influence; a Theory of Poetry* (New York, 1973), p. 61.

2. Ronald A. Rebholz, *The Life of Fulke Greville, First Lord Brooke* (Oxford, 1971), pp. xxxiii-iv.

3. Gary F. Waller, 'Acts of Reading: the Production of Meaning in *Astrophil and Stella*,' *SLI*, 15 (1982), p. 24. See also Arthur Marotti, '"Love is not love": Elizabethan Sonnet Sequences and the Social Order,' *ELH*, 49 (1982), pp. 396-428.

4. *Selected Writings of Fulke Greville*, ed. Joan Rees (London, 1973), pp. 144, 151-2.

5. Quotations from *Caelica* are taken from *Poems and Dramas of Fulke Greville, First Lord Brooke*, ed. Geoffrey Bullough (Edinburgh, 1939), Vol. I; spelling is modernized and punctuation modified.

6. *The Fatal Mirror; Themes and Techniques in the Poetry of Fulke Greville* (Charlottesville, 1972), p. 143.

6. I follow the text of *The Sonnets*, ed. J. Dover Wilson, 2nd edition (Cambridge, 1967). Shakespeare's sonnets are discussed in relation to Sidney's by Inga-Stina Ewbank, 'Sincerity and the Sonnet,' *Essays and Studies*, ed. Anne Barton,

n.s. 34 (1981), pp. 19-44.

8. *Ben Jonson's Literary Criticism*, ed. James D. Redwine, Jr. (Lincoln, 1970), p. 19.

9. I follow the text in John Donne, *The Complete English Poems*, ed. A.J. Smith (Hardmondsworth, 1973), but for a few changes in punctuation.

10. I follow the text in *George Herbert and the Seventeenth Century Religious Poets*, ed. Mario A. Di Cesare (New York, 1978). Margaret Bottrall, *George Herbert* (London, 1954), pp. 119-24, discusses Herbert's affinities with Sidney.

THE CULTURAL POLITICS OF THE *DEFENCE OF POETRY*

Alan Sinfield

The notion that the *Defence of Poetry* is constituted of diverse elements is becoming well established since, in 1972, Gary Waller's article 'This Matching of Contraries' and O.B. Hardison Jr.'s 'Two Voices of Sidney's *Apology*.' But the tendency among critics is still to seek and discover a final achieved coherence. In 1980, D.H. Craig argued that 'Sidney has drawn on traditions that are at odds with each other,' but gestured finally towards a higher level of coherence in the 'humanist spirit of flexibility and clear-sighted purposefulness' through which Sidney constructs 'an engine of persuasion to virtue out of the wide and miscellaneous intellectual inheritance of the Renaissance.' And we find in 1981 Martin N. Raitiere arguing for 'transcending these antinomies and gathering the entire oration into the brilliantly framed work of art we always knew it was.'[1] My paper challenges the transcendent idea of the *Defence* as the critical tradition has always known it. The diverse constituents of the *Defence* reveal an intervention at a particular political juncture, aimed at appropriating literature to earnest protestant activism through a negotiation of the divergent codes of pagan literature and protestantism.

In 1959 C. Wright Mills, in *Power, Politics, and People,* drew attention to 'the cultural apparatus':

> For most of what he calls solid fact, sound interpretation, suitable presentations, every man is increasingly dependent upon the observation posts, the interpretation centres, the presentation depots, which in contemporary society are established by means of what I am going to call the cultural apparatus. This apparatus is composed of all the organisations and *milieux* in which artistic, intellectual and scientific work goes on, and of the means by which work is made available to circles, publics, and masses. . . . Taken as a whole, the cultural apparatus is the lens of mankind through which men

see; the medium by which they interpret and
report what they see.[2]

Louis Althusser's formulation of the ideological state apparatuses--the institutions of religion, education, the family, the law, politics, organized labour, communications and culture--points us, similarly, towards the means by which the reproduction of the relations of production is secured.[3] Wright Mills and Althusser are concerned mainly with the way this works in modern society, but the Elizabethan state had a highly developed cultural apparatus.

Recent study has suggested that Queen Elizabeth spent relatively little on maintaining a culture which would legitimate her own rule, but she was adroit at stimulating others to do this for her.[4] Courtiers sponsored progresses, pageants, tournaments, interludes, masques and plays; portraits and tombs; palaces and houses; music from masses to madrigals; and the whole range of literary forms. Artists were encouraged by patronage to incorporate secular and religious symbolism which ratified the power structure and projected it onto a supernatural dimension. Infringements were censored and punished. The system filtered down through the gentry and was disseminated over the whole country through churches and schools, via the universities and local patronage. It has been suggested that Charles I's failure to sustain an adequately rooted 'national' culture crucially damaged his power.[5]

But culture, like power, is neither monolithic nor static. Althusser remarks that the ruling class holds power 'openly or more often by means of alliances between classes or class factions' (p. 139). The scope for negotiation which this implies has been theorised at Stuart Hall's Centre for Contemporary Cultural Studies:

> The dominant culture of a complex society is
> never a homogeneous structure. It is layered,
> reflecting different interests within the
> dominant class (e.g. an aristocratic versus a
> bourgeois outlook), containing different traces
> from the past (e.g. religious ideas within a
> largely secular culture), as well as emergent
> elements in the present.[6]

The Elizabethan era saw a strengthening of centralised power, a reduction in the financial and military independence of great magnates, a growth in loyalty to and dependence on the Crown and in the importance of Parliament; rebellion became disreputable.[7] But all this increased the scope for *political* manoeuvring between families and factions, and the Reformation made religious allegiance into a specially powerful token of ideological and factional affiliation. Sidney's

Cultural Politics of the Defence

Lady of May was a contribution to the welcoming of the Queen to Leicester's house at Wanstead but it was also, it seems, an attempt to urge an active protestant policy upon Elizabeth. She resisted this implication and chose, against the grain of the entertainment, the cautious shepherd rather than the lively forester.[8] This initial instance points us towards the scope for negotiation which was available to a man like Sidney within the Elizabethan cultural apparatus, and to the kind of intervention to which he was committed.

The cultural apparatus of Elizabethan England was, of course, underpinned by religion: the Church was one of its primary institutions and it exercised considerable control over publishing and education at all levels. However, much of the content of education was, by tradition, pagan, and the humanist movement, by taking seriously the philosophy of classical writers, made this a factor to be reckoned with. Initially humanism and protestantism had been united, often, in their opposition to scholasticism (in the person of Robert Barnes, for instance[9]). But there was a divergence of interests, as Luther at once perceived: 'It grieves me to the heart that this damned, conceited, rascally heathen'--Aristotle--'has with his false words deluded and made fools of so many of the best Christians. God has sent him as a plague upon us for our sins.'[10]

In 1582 the Privy Council ordered that Christopher Ocland's new Latin text-book be used in schools, 'where diverse heathen books are ordinarily read and taught, from which the youth of the realm doth rather receive infection in manners than advancement in virtue.'[11] But such attentions were intermittent; earnest protestants never really grasped this issue. Like Sidney with literature, they preferred to use the existing educational system for their own purposes. Lawrence Stone observes, 'It was this infiltration of the universities which turned Puritanism from the sectional eccentricity of a few great households in the countryside and groups of artisans and small traders in the towns into a nation-wide movement affecting all classes of society.'[12] But this infiltration inevitably involved compromise. The heathens were not forbidden: they were too firmly established--not merely such that protestants could not dislodge them, but that protestants could not envisage the cultural apparatus without them. Calvin in the dedication to his *Commentaries on Genesis* (1563) asserted that Aristotle 'applied whatever skill he possessed to defraud God of his glory,' and that Plato 'corrupted and mingled with so many figments the slender principles of truth which he received, that this fictitious kind of teaching would be rather injurious than profitable'; we should attend to Genesis instead.[13] But within two pages Calvin is enthusing about the humanistic attainment of the ten-year-old Henry of Navarre: 'liberal instruction has been superadded to chaste discipline. Already imbued with the rudiments of literature, you have not cast away (as nearly all are wont to do) these studies in disgust, but still advance with alacrity in the cultivation of your genius' (I,xlvii). We cannot tell how far the inconsistency is produced by Calvin's unquenchable respect for the classics and how far he is deferring to the existing cultural apparatus in the crucially important court of Navarre.

What we can see, is that the relationship between protestantism and classical literature within the cultural apparatus was an issue for negotiation. It is upon this site that Sidney conducts his defence. The concern of a man of his class and interests with literature was not novel: the sixteenth century saw a steady development of the assumption that a gentleman should be educated. Nor was anxiety about pagan writing unprecedented for Christians (Petrarch, for instance). But the Reformation intensified such problems by stressing the coherence and direction of religious doctrine, and a heightened awareness of the problem of pagan letters followed. As we shall see shortly, aspects of these questions were perceived and handled by Sidney in ways which are distinctively protestant, and we shall understand him best as part of a faction committed to reinforcing the influence of protestantism within the cultural apparatus and the state generally.[14]

The main anxieties about pagan writing concerned the gods, love, heroism, and human capacity in a fallen world. The first two came together in respect of the gods. One strategy was to insist upon exclusively allegorical interpretation. Thomas Wilson asserts in *The Art of Rhetoric* (1553):

> undoubtedly there is no one tale among all the
> poets, but under the same is comprehended some
> thing that pertaineth either to the amendment
> of manners, to the knowledge of truth, to the
> setting forth of Nature's work, or else to the
> understanding of some notable thing done. (fol. 104r)

We may see that this large claim is supposed to justify especially the sexual escapades of the gods from Wilson's examples: Jupiter's assault on Danae shows that women will be won with money, his changing into a bull to abduct Isis that beauty may overcome the beast (fol. 104v). The argument is traditional enough (though the earnest protestant will not use the medieval device of theological allegory, only moral allegory), but Wilson's insistence shows that he is struggling to make a case. Arthur Golding in the preface and epistle to his translation of Ovid's *Metamorphoses* (1567) tries to justify the stories through ethical allegory; on the title page he warns, 'with skill, heed, and judgement, this work must be read,/For else to the reader it stands in small stead.'

Thomas Becon is more straightforward in his *Cathechism*

(1560). After 'the word of god,' the schoolmaster will teach

> good letters, I mean poets, orators, historiographers, philosophers, &c. . . . But, in reading these kinds of authors to his disciples, the school-master must diligently take heed that he read those only to his scholars that be most profitable and contain in them no matter that may either hinder the religion of God or the innocency of manners. Such writers in many places of their works are wanton and unhonest, as Martialis, Catullus, Tibullus, Propertius, Cornelius Gallus, and such-like; some wicked and ungodly, as Lucianus, &c.[15]

Sidney handles the issue of the gods rather well. His division of poetry into three kinds--divine, philosophical and (the type he mainly discusses) 'that feigning notable images of virtues, vices, or what else' (*Misc. Prose* 81.36-7)[16] --enables him to bracket off religious matters. He gives the divine poet the greatest honour, and in expounding the category adds biblical examples to Scaliger's list, keeping pagan instances for a derogatory parenthesis. He does not, like Plato, Scaliger and the Pléiade, claim heavenly inspiration for the poet; he does not, like Puttenham in the opening paragraph of his *Art of English Poesy* (1589), draw an unqualified analogy between the poet and God. Like Sir Thomas Elyot, he employs to the general credit of poetry the fact that the Romans called any poet a *vates*, but he is not comfortable with it: he insists that the use of Virgil for fortune-telling was 'a very vain and godless superstition,' and verse in oracles only seemed to have divine force (76.35-77.8). He invokes the psalms, but at once denies any profane implication. A problem remains: such attention to divine poetry approaches the position of protestants like du Bartas, who rejected secular poetry altogether. Sidney observes that psalm singing 'is used with the fruit of comfort by some, when, in sorrowful pangs of their death-bringing sins, they find the consolation of the never-leaving goodness' (80.15-8). This seems to echo the preface to Sternhold and Hopkins' metrical version of the psalms (1562), but notice the corollary which they draw: psalms are 'to be used of all sorts of people privately for their solace and comfort: laying apart all ungodly songs and ballads which tend only to the nourishing of vice and corrupting of youth.' Sidney's reply to this is only that it follows 'very unwillingly, that good is not good, because better is better' (102.12-3).

Sidney eventually confronts directly the argument about the gods in pagan poetry:

> the poets did not induce such opinions, but did imitate those opinions already induced. For all

> the Greek stories can well testify that the very
> religion of that time stood upon many and many-
> fashioned gods, not taught so by the poets, but
> followed according to their nature of imitation.
> (108.11-5)

Sidney manifests here an awareness of ideological context, and hence of cultural change, that is notably absent from the main part of his theory.

On love poetry Sidney is less secure. He suppresses it from his definitions of elegy and lyric--the former is taken solely as lament, ignoring Ovid and the latin elegists; the latter is said to give moral precepts and natural problems and to praise virtue and sometimes God. However, Sidney knows that this is partial, and not only in respect of those genres. As he admits later on, 'They say, the comedies rather teach than reprehend amorous conceits. They say the lyric is larded with passionate sonnets; the elegiac weeps the want of his mistress; and that even to the heroical, Cupid hath ambitiously climbed' (103.32-5). The answer to this is highly indirect. Sidney grants two objections whilst hinting at parenthetical reservations, but his appeals to 'love and beauty' and 'philosophers' support only Platonic love. Finally he grants that lust, vanity and scurrility possess much love poetry--but yet that we may 'not say that poetry abuseth man's wit, but that man's wit abuseth poetry' (104.12-3). Poetry generally is vindicated at the expense of most love poetry. And later on he declares that songs and sonnets of love might better be devoted to 'the immortal goodness of that God who giveth us hands to write and wits to conceive' (116.31-2).

That Sidney's caution is not the standard currency of Elizabethan critical thought may be observed through comparison with some less earnest writers. Puttenham is openly liberal. He says poetry provides instruction but sees it also as 'the common solace of mankind in all his travails and cares of this transitory life.' As such it may 'allowably bear matter not always of the gravest, or of any great commodity or profit, but rather in some sort, vain, dissolute, or wanton, so it be not very scandalous and of evil example.' Sir John Harington in the preface to his translation of *Orlando Furioso* (1591) is arch and knowing. He rehearses Sidney's arguments about the teaching power of literature, but on love he is jovial:

> As for the pastoral with the sonnet or epigram,
> though many times they savour of wantonness and
> love and toying, and, now and then breaking the
> rules of poetry, go into plain scurrility, yet
> even the worst of them may be not ill applied,
> and are, I must confess, too delightful.

He reckons that even the blushing matron will read them when no observer is by.[17]

Sidney engages in manipulations over the gods and love poetry because he is determined to appropriate classical writing to protestant purposes. To the texts he discusses we may apply Terry Eagleton's comment on Richardson's novels: they are part of an ideological struggle, 'pitched standards around which battle is joined, instruments which help to constitute social interests.' Sidney is piecing together divergent discourses--defending secular writing in earnest protestant terms. The effect is characteristic of the way ideologies are developed: 'The process of ideological elaboration is thus closer . . . to Lévi-Strauss' process of *bricolage*, than it is to the consistent elaboration of theoretical or philosophical "world views,"' says Stuart Hall. Ideologies 'will frequently be extended and amplified to deal with new situations by "putting together," often in an illogical or incoherent way, what were, previously, the fragments of more ordered or stable meaning-systems.'[18] Sidney's argument is problematic because he is 'putting together' diverse elements within an unsettled cultural apparatus.

Doubtless this was, for Sidney, a necessary personal negotiation: he needed to accommodate divergent commitments. Also, we may discern a purposeful intervention. Sidney aims to tilt the cultural apparatus towards protestantism by making literature work for protestantism and, conversely, making protestantism central in responses to literature. Of course, this was not his project alone. 'In acquiring one's conception of the world one belongs to a particular grouping which is that of all the social elements which share the same mode of thinking and acting,' Gramsci observes.[19] We should associate Sidney with other prominent supporters of the puritan faction: his uncles, the Earls of Leicester and Warwick; the Earl of Huntingdon, an uncle by marriage whom Sidney appointed one of the supervisors of his will; the Earl of Bedford (author of ten folio volumes of theological reflections); the Earl of Pembroke who married Sidney's sister; Sir Francis Walsingham, whose daughter Sidney married; Sir Walter Mildmay (founder of Emmanuel College, Cambridge); Sir Francis Knollys. These men amounted to a faction determined to defend and perhaps develop the reformed religion in England. It was in their interest to do this, but they were sustained by a specific ideological formation. The Calvinist conception of the godly aristocrat or gentleman helps us to understand Sidney and his purpose in the *Defence*, and returns us to that text and its treatment of epic heroism and the provenance of poetry.

Michael Walzer has shown how, under pressure of social and religious change, the roles of the old knight and Renaissance courtier were becoming untenable. The monarch's function was being redefined in terms of absolute power and the administration of the country was becoming more sophisticated. If the gentleman was to retain an independent and significant position, he could no longer rely on feudal status or military prowess. He needed to emphasise his social and civil function, and this could be most effectively sustained upon a religious basis. Walzer believes that Sidney, with his friend du Plessis-Mornay, suggested an 'ideal alternative to the courtier: animated by a fine sense of personal virtue, they were conditioned at the same time by a new Calvinist zeal.' So Sidney urged his brother to develop his powers: 'your purpose is, being a gentleman born, to furnish yourself with the knowledge of such things as may be serviceable to your country and fit for your calling.'[20] Being a gentleman is not enough by itself; observe the specifically protestant concept of the calling, which invested social responsibility with religious zeal.

The point was often pressed upon Sidney. Languet urged him to put his powers 'in the service of your country, and of all good men; since you are only the steward of this gift, you will wrong Him who conferred such a great benefit on you if you prove to have abused it.' In the dedication of his *History of Wales* to Sidney in 1584 the Bishop of St. Asaph reminded him that he must eventually render an account of the use of his talents and should therefore devote them to God and his country.[21] Sidney's French Huguenot friends theorised the matter--Francis Hotman in his *Franco-Gallia* (1573) and du Plessis-Mornay in his *Vindiciae contra tyrannos* (1576).

Lawrence Humphrey, president of Magdalen College, Oxford, expounded this conception of the role of the gentry in *The Nobles* (1563). In a way Humphrey anticipates the *Defence of Poetry*, for he insists on the importance of education and recommends many secular authors. But he is less prepared to compromise than Sidney: he rejects the *Aeneid* because it presents unChristian values too eloquently, and complains that too many read 'human things, not divine, love toys, not fruitful lessons, Venus' games, not weighty studies tending to increase of godliness, dignity, or true and sound commodity' (sig. y, x). Humphrey's gentleman or aristocrat is to be precisely trained for his godly responsibilities.

These considerations seem to have shaped, or rather validated, Sidney's career. A primary task was the support of zealous ministers: Humphrey insists, 'this is peculiar to noblemen, to relieve the cause of the gospel fainting and falling, to strengthen with their aid impoverished religion, to shield it forsaken with their patronage' (sig. m). We know of three instances where Sidney did this. In 1575 he was consulted by his father about a tutor for his brother at Oxford. Robert Dorsett was appointed, and gained permission to associate John Buste with him. We can deduce Buste's puritan orientation from his dispute with the people of Ludlow in 1582, when he was parson there. Whitgift (then Bishop of

Worcester) reported that the congregation had been accused of insufficient godliness and implied that Buste had been too zealous: 'Truly they are a good people, and lovers of God's word, for any thing that I learn to the contrary. But many of us have zeal without discretion, and salt without peace; the principal cause of the variance and dissention in many places.'[22]

In 1582 Sidney appointed as his chaplain James Stile, who had attracted the attention of the authorities by preaching outside his parish in 1574 and whose living was sequestered in 1575. In 1576 and 1579 he resigned parishes to take lecturing posts, which were beyond the control of the bishops. After Sidney's death he lectured again and then became Walsingham's chaplain. And Sidney called to his deathbed George Gifford who had been deprived of his living at Maldon in 1584 for resisting Whitgift's injunction to subscribe to a statement accepting the prayer book; Whitgift rejected an appeal by Burghley on his behalf because Gifford seemed to be 'a ringleader of the rest.'[23]

As well as supporting the gospel at home, the gentleman was to work for a protestant foreign policy. Walzer invokes 'the vision of a Protestant nation presided over by an elite of godly aristocrats waging chivalric warfare for God's glory, born in the mind of a man like Sir Philip Sidney' (*The Revolution of the Saints*, p. 16). It was Sidney's zeal in this cause which limited his career as a statesman. It seems that he exceeded his brief on his embassy to the Palatine in 1577 -- the Queen had no enthusiasm for a protestant league which might lead to expense and war. *The Lady of May*, the tennis court quarrel (1579) and the Letter to Queen Elizabeth (1579) all show him risking the royal displeasure in his insistence upon an earnest protestant policy. Fulke Greville says that Sidney, like William of Orange, 'never divided the consideration of estate from the cause of religion.'[24] We see the tenor of Sidney's commitment in a letter to Walsingham from the Netherlands about his difficulties:

> in my heart the love of the cause doth so far overbalance them all, that with God's grace they shall never make me weary of my resolution . . . . I know not whether I am deceived, but I am faithfully persuaded that if [the Queen] should withdraw herself other springs would rise to help this action. For methinks I see the great work indeed in hand, against the abusers of the world.

Sidney's literary work was his response to the Queen's refusal to use him seriously between 1577 and 1585. He wrote to Languet in 1578, 'to what purpose should our thoughts be directed to various kinds of knowledge unless room be afforded for putting it into practice so that public advantage may be the result--which in a corrupt age we cannot hope for?'[25] Sidney found the best answer he could, and decided to do cultural work for the cause.

'It is impossible to understand the concrete utterance without accustoming oneself to its values, without understanding the orientation of its evaluations in the ideological environment,' wrote M.M. Bakhtin.[26] Placing Sidney's work in the ideological environment I have proposed is both stimulating and problematic.[27] Emphasis upon the responsibility of the gentleman to society and a religious cause, and upon humble acknowledgement that any achievement is God's, is not compatible with the amoral, personal prowess which characterises the epic hero; indeed, any human capacity comes into question, as we shall see in respect of the provenance of the poet's vision.

Elsewhere I have described the careers of Musidorus and Pyrocles as 'a fantasy upon the heroic protestant action against Spanish policy in Europe and the New World which Sidney sought to undertake but the Queen would not permit.'[28] Yet this heroism is challenged in the *New Arcadia*. Musidorus and Pyrocles seem to be the perfect princes, but their love slides towards lust, they are unable to defeat Amphialus and it seems that they have much to learn from the princesses. The characters are subjected to suffering, impotence and failure, and seem to be developing a more inward and spiritual strength, based on a knowledge of their limitations. As in *The Fairy Queen* and *Paradise Lost* (though with different consequences in each case), heroism is problematised in a zealously protestant ideological environment.

In narrative, such issues can be worked through and adjusted, and apparent resolutions can be arranged (though the *New Arcadia* is unfinished). But in a reasoned argument they are liable to produce strains and inconsistencies. As well as the gods and love, Sidney in the *Defence* has to deal with the heroic values of pagan epic poetry. William Perkins sets out a vigorous protestant position in *The Cases of Conscience* (1600):

> the Philosopher calls *Magnanimity* (whereby a man thinks himself worthy of great honours, and thereupon enterpriseth great things) a virtue; which notwithstanding is to beholden a flat vice. For by the Law of God, every man is to range himself within the limits of his calling, and not to dare once to go out of it. Whereas, on the contrary, the scope and end of this virtue (as they term it) is to make men attempt high and great matters above their reach, and so to go beyond their callings. Besides, it is directly opposite to the virtue of humility, which teacheth that a man ought always to be base, vile and lowly in his own eyes.

Cultural Politics of the Defence

This was not a new point--Machiavelli made it, though with the opposite evaluation of the alternatives:

> Our religion has glorified humble and contemplative men, rather than men of action. It has assigned as man's highest good, humility, abnegation, and contempt for mundane things, whereas that other hath identified it with magnanimity, bodily strength, and everything else that conduces to make men bold.[29]

Here again, the issue is not a uniquely protestant one, but protestant suspicion of any claims that might be made for human achievement in a fallen world rendered it specially provocative.

Sidney responds by trying to redefine 'magnanimity' so that it will be less objectionable. In his account of 'the Heroical' he says it 'maketh magnanimity and justice shine,' adding the second quality--justice--to bring the description nearer to Christian values. He then offers the noticeably vaguer claims that epic instills 'virtue' and 'inflameth the mind with desire to be worthy.' Then he gives two instances of Aeneas, both of them chosen more for their protestant appeal than their precision in characterising epic--'how he governeth himself in the ruin of his country; in the preserving his old father, and carrying away his religious ceremonies; in obeying God's commandment to leave Dido' (*Misc. Prose*, 98.17-9). Humphrey, as I have said, condemned the *Aeneid* because it presented pagan values too eloquently; Harington justifies the sexual license in *Orlando Furioso* by invoking Aeneas' lapse with Dido. At another point Sidney declares that, hearing 'the tales of Hercules, Achilles, Cyrus, Aeneas,' one 'must needs hear the right description of wisdom, valour, and justice' (92.21). Surely this approximation, blatantly designed to appropriate epic heroes for Christian virtues, obliges us to concede a point against Sidney in favour of Stephen Gosson, who in his *School of Abuse* (1579) remarks that Maximus Tyrius defends Homer by 'wresting the rashness of Ajax to valour, the cowardice of Ulysses to policy, the dotage of Nestor to grave counsel.'[30] Sidney's material reveals its intractability.

The boldest move in the *Defence* is the account of the provenance of the poet's vision. I have quoted Perkins' statement that 'every man is to range himself within the limits of his calling'; Sidney says that the poet alone is found 'freely ranging only within the zodiac of his own wit' (78.29-30). The main competitors to poetry are restricted severely by the lapsed condition of humanity. History, 'being captivated to the truth of a foolish world, is many times a terror from well-doing, and an encouragement to unbridled wickedness' (90.13-5): the history of a fallen world shows the wicked triumphing and does not incite to virtue. The drawback of philosophy also is that it does not entice fallen people to virtue: 'to be moved to do that which we know, or to be moved with desire to know, *hoc opus, hic labor est*' (91.33-4)--Sidney denies the optimistic assumption of rationalist humanism, that the good is naturally desirable. But the poet seems to be unhampered.

Sidney claims extraordinary scope for poets, including pagans--that they transcend fallen nature and 'grow in effect another nature, in making things either better than nature bringeth forth, or, quite anew, forms such as never were in nature' (78.24-6). There are two possible protestant rationales for this. Sidney has set up one of them by his threefold division of poets, for the ethical insight attributed to the main kind was, according to protestants, entirely within the competence of pagan reason. 'Nothing, indeed, is more common,' Calvin allows, 'than for man to be sufficiently instructed in a right course of conduct by natural law.'[31] So Sidney remarks that 'in nature we know it is well to do well, and what is well, and what is evil,' adding, 'I speak still of human, and according to the human conceit' (91.33-6). It is not morals, but matters affecting salvation which are beyond the competence of pagans, and they are set aside as the province of divine poetry. Sidney uses the distinction in his letter of 22 May 1580 to Edward Denny: the scriptures 'are certainly the incomparable lantern in this fleshly darkness of ours. . . . To them if you will add as to the help of the second table (I mean that which contains the love of thy neighbour, and dealing betwixt man and man) some parts of moral philosophy, I think you shall do very wisely.'[32]

This principle would justify a certain attention to pagan writing--it is used by Becon and Humphrey. But Sidney uses also a second rationale, for he wants to incorporate the larger claims for poetry made by humanists. Hence the exalted tone of his account of 'the poet, disdaining to be tied to any such subjection, lifted up with the vigour of his own invention' (78.22-4). This sounds so ambitious for fallen humanity that Sidney must at once 'give right honour to the heavenly Maker of that maker' and acknowledge 'that first accursed fall of Adam.' So he declares that 'our erected wit maketh us know what perfection is, and yet our infected will keepeth us from reaching unto it' (79.19-26).

Modern critics have seized upon this latter formula as a triumphant reconciliation of humanism and Christianity--as somehow saving both humanity's intellectual aspirations and its postlapsarian degradation. It is evidence of Sidney's wish to do that, but it deposits him strangely between the two stools of protestant thought. His idea of the scope of the reason is Hooker's not Calvin's; but the recalcitrance of the will is Calvin's position, not Hooker's.[33] Sidney's poet meets the criteria of neither of the main contemporary versions of protestantism: he is more fallen than is allowed in the one, less than in the other.

Although he violates the logic of Calvinism, Sidney perhaps manifests a typical paradox of the puritan mind. Perry Miller observes that the doctrine of total depravity 'ought to have forced man to grovel in the dust, but instead one of its principal effects was a renewed emphasis upon the importance of his role in the creation, a fresh vision of the boundless possibilities of his genius.' So even Calvin declares, in respect of our ethical capacity, that we should 'with our whole soul aspire to heaven' and 'endeavour to show forth the glory of God,' trying to 'attain to goodness itself.' Miller explains, 'The more the people were informed concerning the ravages of original sin, the more distinctly they came to know the lineaments of nobility and worth.' Something like this movement is actually present in the *Defence*, in the gnomic statement that the power of the poet to transcend fallen nature affords 'no small arguments to the credulous of that first accursed fall of Adam' (79.23-4). This is the same kind of flip between degeneration and perfection. In fact it is anticipated by Calvin, when he remarks that 'it is impossible to think of our primeval dignity without being immediately reminded of the sad spectacle of our ignominy and corruption, ever since we fell from our original in the person of our first parent.'34

This second rationale for the specially exalted capacity of the poet may, then, be compatible with the spirit of protestantism, though not with the letter. And Sidney thus seems to achieve a reconciliation between earnest protestantism and the most elevated humanist conception of poetry--a triumphant merger guaranteeing control of the cultural apparatus. The problem is, that the erected wit, as I have expounded it, must surely be a property of the devout Christian--as when William Perkins declares that the converted sinner experiences 'a renewing and restoring of that purity and holiness which was lost by man's fall, with the abolishment of that corruption that is in all the powers of the soul.'35 As such, it cannot be a property of pagan poetry. Of Sidney's two rationales, therefore, the first justifies all poetry, though not at a very exalted pitch; the second, at a most exalted pitch, justifies Christian poetry but not the pagan writing which figured so largely in the Elizabethan cultural apparatus. The co-occurrence of the two rationales effects a confusion which gives the impression of a far more comprehensive harmonisation of protestant principles and pagan writings than has in fact been achieved.

The final topic which demands attention is Sidney's insistence that characters in literature represent absolute moral qualities: nature has not produced 'so true a lover as Theagenes, so constant a friend as Pylades, so valiant a man as Orlando, so right a prince as Xenophon's Cyrus, so excellent a man every way as Virgil's Aeneas' (79.1-4). Thus he simplifies fictional characters into abstractions, refusing to admit the existence of mixed or developing characters and the controversies they provoke--such as I have mentioned in relation to Orlando and Aeneas; and such as we experience in Sidney's *Arcadia* and *Astrophil and Stella*.

Sidney perhaps does this because he wishes to approximate his theory to neoclassicism. Tasso asserted in his *Discourses on the Heroic Poem* that 'epic illustriousness is based on lofty military valour and the magnanimous resolve to die, on piety, religion, and deeds alight with these virtues.' But Tasso does not extend this idealisation to tragedy, which he contrasts, as showing characters 'fallen through some error into unhappiness.' An awareness that tragedy poses special problems is apparent in Seneca's Elizabethan editor, Thomas Newton, who sought to deny that the plays tend 'sometime to the praise of ambition, sometime to the maintenance of cruelty, now and then to the approbation of incontinency, and here and there to the ratification of tyranny.'36 But Sidney is determined to impose his absolute ethical structures upon tragedy also: 'If the poet do his part aright, he will show you in Tantalus, Atreus, and such like, nothing that is not to be shunned; in Cyrus, Aeneas, Ulysses, each thing to be followed.' And again: 'if evil men come to the stage, they ever go out (as the tragedy writer answered to one that misliked the show of such persons) so manacled as they little animate folks to follow them' (90.10-3). But Atreus is left triumphant (though perhaps mad), and Medea; and what of Hercules?

Sidney's determination to discover absolute moral exemplifications in all literature seems to be in part a consequence of his commitment to the argument that poetry is justified by its ethical structure. Even more, it seems to be the corollary of his idealised view of the provenance of poetry, as deriving from the erected wit which transcends the fallen condition. Figures in a prelapsarian idea can hardly be partly good and partly bad; they would not carry 'an apparent shining' (86.21-2). Sidney is obliged to follow through the implications of his theory, and it leads him into partial reading which disregards the actuality of pagan literature.

Anthony Giddens proposes that the three principal ideological forms are 'the representation of sectional interests as universal ones' and 'the denial or transmutation of contradictions' and 'the naturalisation of the present.'37 Sidney in the *Defence* manifests all three. Despite his awareness that pagan gods are what we should expect in pagan society, he naturalises the present to the extent that no difference in ethical values between protestants and pagans is acknowledged. To do this, he denies or transmutes the contradictions within pagan literature and between that literature and his society.

And his aim is to construct a relationship between the cultural apparatus and a particular faction in Elizabethan politics, but this is not admitted: sectional interests are represented as universal ones. The historical specificity of pagan literature is effaced as Sidney appropriates it to promote earnest protestantism within the cultural apparatus.

Sidney himself was at once caught up in the same kind of ideological process by protestant activists, who represented their sectional interests as universal and denied or transmuted contradictions in Sidney's life. They appropriated Sidney in the same way that he did fictional characters, as a notable image of virtue. Arthur Golding in his dedication of *The Trueness of the Christian Religion* (1587) to Leicester declared that Sidney died 'the honourablest death that could be desired, and best beseeming a Christian knight, whereby he hath worthily won to himself immortal fame among the godly, and left example worthy of imitation to others of his calling.' Fulke Greville was uneasy about justifying any poetry, but insofar as he was prepared to do that, he followed Sidney's proposal; hence he interprets *Arcadia* as offering 'moral images and examples, as directing threads to guide every man through the confused labyrinth of his own desires and life.' And Greville claims Sidney himself as the same kind of ideal pattern: his life of true worth 'did, by way of example, far exceed the pictures of it in any moral precepts.'[38] This is just what Sidney says about how the poet constructs his characters: 'whatsoever the philosopher saith should be done, he giveth a perfect picture of it in someone by whom he presupposeth it was done' (85.22-4).

The process did not end with Sidney's society. Shelley co-opted him as one of the 'inheritors of unfulfilled renown' who welcome Adonais to his 'winged throne'--

> Sidney, as he fought
> And as he fell and as he lived and loved
> Sublimely mild, a Spirit without spot.

Yeats invoked Sidney to dignify the quite different life and death of 'Our Sidney and our perfect man' ('In Memory of Major Robert Gregory'). Sir Arthur Quiller-Couch offered Sidney to his students at Cambridge as a model--a 'perfect young knight' who combined a literary sensibility and 'bodily games' (as witnessed in *Astrophil and Stella* 41), adding:

> perhaps no Englishman ever lived more graciously
> or, having used life, made a better end. But you
> have seen this morning's newspaper: you have read of
> Captain Scott and his comrades, and in particular of
> the death of Captain Oates; and you know that the
> breed of Sidney is not extinct. Gentlemen, let us
> keep our language noble: for we still have heroes

Cultural Politics of the Defence

to commemorate!³⁹

Modern criticism has all too often engaged in similarly ideological appropriations of Sidney. As John Fekete says, the great tendency of the twentieth-century critical tradition is to construct 'a totality without struggle and historical movement.'⁴⁰ A version which prevailed for a while is John Buxton's:

> For himself, the hard clarity of Calvin's logic suited him, as did a similar quality in the mind of Ramus; but in poetry he never made the mistake that so many Puritans make, of emphasising the *utile*, the propaganda, at the expense of the *dulce*, the delight . . . . Sidney was much too civilised a man to fall into the ancient heresy of demanding that poetry should be 'socially engaged,' of insisting that the poet should accept his readers' dogmas and prejudices.⁴¹

Buxton's major work on Sidney's circle and patronage provide in many ways the basis for the account of him in this paper as intervening in the Elizabethan cultural apparatus. But without the political and religious commitment, Buxton's picture is damagingly partial, and surely the evidence is against him--bearing in mind the translations of the psalms, du Plessis-Mornay and du Bartas, and what Sidney said he was doing, and what Greville said he was doing. Buxton's own 'dogmas and prejudices' lead him to recruit Sidney to his viewpoint--and, of course, that viewpoint is then naturalised (these engaged chaps push prejudices whereas civilised people just tell the truth). More recent interpretations of Sidney's work, whilst appearing to abandon the preoccupation with unity and effacement of struggle (with or without Buxton's Oxford gentlemanly orientation) may nevertheless construct a (deconstructed) depoliticised Sidney.

This account of Sidney's ideological manoeuvres is not meant as a complacent attack on our benighted forebears, though a distrust of Sidney's powers and purposes is perhaps salutary. It is merely to see the *Defence* not as an elegant selection from current commonplaces (who would bother to write that?), but as an intervention at a particular cultural and political conjuncture--like Wordsworth's Preface to *Lyrical Ballads* or Eliot's 'Tradition and the Individual Talent.' Moreover, the strategies Sidney adopts in his attempt to negotiate a relationship between the cultural apparatus and his political faction are not without relevance for those who would do the same today. His appropriation of prestigious cultural tokens and enthusiasm for images of virtue constitutes one set of possibilities for getting literature (or any cultural form) to speak the kinds of meanings one prefers.

And, as we have seen, Sidney has been used in this way. The drawbacks of such a practice are what they were in Sidney's time: that in so far as the preferred meaning is insisted upon it is liable to be rejected, and in so far as it is left implicit it is liable to be incorporated into dominant meanings. One would do better with the procedure Sidney himself adopts over the pagan gods ('the very religion *of that time*' --108.13)--acknowledging and exploring difference in its historical and ideological dimensions.

The decay of one attempt to appropriate literary forms by insisting upon exemplary images may be observed in the theory of Soviet realism. This is now, of course, central to the cultural apparatus of the U.S.S.R., but it happens to be the closest current approximation to Sidney's theory. Leonid Brezhnev in his *Report to the XXVI Congress* (1981) expressed satisfaction that 'vivid images of our contemporaries' in cultural work 'move people, prompt debates, and make people think of the present and the future.' This thought-provoking role for literature we might endorse, but Brezhnev also betrays an ideological inconsistency, for his main emphasis is not on prompting debate, but on presenting an exemplary heroic ideal:

> The works of authors devoted to the military theme foster love of country and staunchness in hardship. . . . The heroes of these works are people from different walks of life: a building team leader, a collective-farm chairman, a railway worker, an army officer, a pilot, or an eminent scientist. But in each of them the reader or the viewer sees his own thoughts and feelings, and the embodiment of the finest qualities of the Soviet character.[42]

In the name of the supposed achievements and permanence of Soviet society rather than the supposed perfection of the prelapsarian condition, and with a different set of heroes, some of the same virtues are absolutized as in the *Defence*, and the same exemplary role is assigned to literature. Both theorists efface the historical specificity of creative writing, and both restrict grossly, in the interest of a particular view of culture and society, the range of attitudes it might express.

Intellectuals now seek a purposeful, creative and critical relationship with the cultural apparatus, trying to avoid the ideological forms manifested by Sir Philip Sidney and General Secretary Brezhnev. This paper has attempted that, aspiring explicitly to historical specificity and to contemporary relevance.

NOTES
   1. G.F. Waller, '"This Matching of Contraries": Bruno, Calvin and the Sidney Circle,' *Neophilologus*, 56 (1972), pp.

331-43; O.B. Hardison, Jr., 'The Two Voices of Sidney's *Apology for Poetry*,' *ELR*, 2 (1972), pp. 83-99; D.H. Craig, 'The Hybrid Growth: Sidney's Theory of Poetry in *An Apology for Poetry*,' *ELR*, 10 (1930), pp. 183-201; Martin N. Raitiere, 'The Unity of Sidney's *Apology for Poetry*,' *SEL*, 21 (1981), pp. 37-58.

2. C. Wright Mills, *Power, Politics, and People*, ed. Irving Louis Horowitz (New York, 1963), p. 406.

3. 'Ideology and Ideological State Apparatuses' in Louis Althusser, *Lenin and Philosophy*, translated by Ben Brewster, 2nd edition., 1977.

4. Malcolm Smuts, 'The Political Failure of Stuart Cultural Patronage' in *Patronage in the Renaissance*, ed. Guy Fitch Lytle and Stephen Orgel (Princeton, 1981), pp. 183-5. See also Eleanor Rosenberg, *Leicester: Patron of Letters* (New York, 1955), ch. 1.

5. Smuts, pp. 183-5.

6. John Clarke, Stuart Hall, Tony Jefferson, Brian Roberts, 'Subcultures, Cultures and Class,' in *Resistance Through Rituals*, ed. Stuart Hall and Tony Jefferson (London, 1976), p. 12.

7. See Lawrence Stone, *The Crisis of the Aristocracy, 1558-1641* (Oxford, 1965), pp. 257-68.

8. See Louis A. Montrose, 'Celebration and Insinuation: Sir Philip Sidney and the Motives of Elizabethan Courtship,' *RenD*, 8 (1977), pp. 3-35; Marie Axton, 'The Tudor Mask and Elizabethan Court Drama,' in *English Drama: Forms and Development*, ed. Marie Axton and Raymond Williams (Cambridge, 1977), pp. 38-42.

9. See Joan Simon, *Education and Society in Tudor England* (Cambridge, 1966), pp. 87-9.

10. *An Open Letter to the Christian Nobility* (1520) in Martin Luther, *Three Treatises* (Philadelphia, 1960), p. 93. See also Stephen Orgel, 'The Royal Theatre and the Role of King' in *Patronage in the Renaissance*, ed. Lytle and Orgel, pp. 263-5.

11. Quoted by Simon, p. 324. See also M.M. Knappen, *Tudor Puritanism* (Chicago, 1939), ch. 26.

12. Stone, pp. 740-1.

13. John Calvin, *Commentaries on the First Book of Moses called Genesis*, Translated by the Rev. John King, 2 vols, (Edinburgh, 1847), I, xlix.

14. See Alan Sinfield, *Literature in Protestant England, 1560-1660* (London, 1983), especially chapters 2, 3. Aspects of this theme are treated by Waller ('"This Matching of Contraries"') and by Andrew D. Weiner in *Sir Philip Sidney and the Poetics of Protestantism* (Minneapolis, 1978), ch. 1.

15. Thomas Becon, *The Cathechism*, ed. John Ayre (Cambridge, 1844), p. 382.

16. On divine poetry see Alan Sinfield, 'Sidney and du Bartas,' *CL*, 27 (1975), pp. 8-20.

17. George Puttenham, *The Arte of English Poesie*, ed. Gladys Doidge Willcock and Alice Walker (Cambridge, 1936), p. 227. Harington in Smith, *Elizabethan Critical Essays*, II, p. 209. See further T.G.A. Nelson, 'Sir John Harington as a Critic of Sir Philip Sidney,' *SP*, LXVII (1970), pp. 41-56.

18. Terry Eagleton, *The Rape of Clarissa* (Oxford, 1982), p. 4; Stuart Hall, 'Deviance, Politics, and the Media,' in *Deviance and Social Control*, ed. Paul Rock and Mary McIntosh (London, 1974), p. 293.

19. Antonio Gramsci, *Selections from the Prison Notebooks*, ed. and translated by Quintin Hoare and Geoffrey Nowell-Smith (London, 1971), p. 324. For Leicester's role in sustaining a puritan wing of the cultural apparatus see Eleanor Rosenberg, *Leicester: Patron of Letters*, ch. 6.

20. Michael Walzer, *The Revolution of the Saints* (New York, 1968), p. 241; *The Prose Works of Sir Philip Sidney*, ed. Albert Feuillerat, 4 vols. (Cambridge, 1963), III, p. 125.

21. Quoted from Osborn, p. 204; John Strype, *Annals of the Reformation* (Oxford, 1824), vol. II, part 1, pp. 403-4.

22. John Strype, *The Life and Acts of John Whitgift*, 3 vols. (Oxford, 1822), I, 198-9. See Osborn, *Young Philip Sidney*, pp. 313-17.

23. See Paul S. Seaver, *The Puritan Lectureships* (Stanford, 1970), pp. 150, 211; Patrick Collinson, *The Elizabethan Puritan Movement* (London, 1967), pp. 265, 267, 279, 374-8.

24. Greville, *Life*, p. 27; see Osborn, *Young Philip Sidney*, especially pp. 496-501; Roger Howell, *Sir Philip Sidney* (London, 1968), chapters 1, 2, 3; Weiner, *Sidney and the Poetics of Protestantism*, pp. 3-8, 18-28.

25. *Prose Works*, III, pp. 119, 166; translated by Malcolm Wallace, *The Life of Sir Philip Sidney* (Cambridge, 1915), p. 198.

26. M.M. Bakhtin and P.N. Medvedev, *The Formal Method in Literary Scholarship* (Baltimore and London, 1978), p. 121.

27. See my articles attempting this in relation to *Astrophil and Stella*: 'Astrophil's Self Deception,' and 'Sidney and Astrophil,' both op. cit.

28. Alan Sinfield, 'Sidney, du Plessis-Mornay and the Pagans,' *PQ*, LVIII (1979), pp. 26-39.

29. *William Perkins*, ed. Thomas F. Merrill (Nieukoop, 1966), p. 165; Niccolò Machiavelli, *The Discourses*, ed. Bernard Crick (Harmondsworth, 1970), p. 278.

30. *Elizabethan Critical Essays*, II, pp. 214-5; Stephen Gosson, *The School of Abuse* (London, 1841), p. 11.

31. John Calvin, *Calvin's Institutes* [translated by Henry Beveridge] (Florida, n.d.), II.ii.22.

32. Printed by Osborn, *Young Philip Sidney*, p. 538. The limits of pagan understanding are the theme of du Plessis-Mornay's *Trueness of the Christian Religion*, which Sidney began to translate; see Alan Sinfield, 'Sidney, du Plessis-Mornay and the Pagans.'

33. Richard Hooker, *Of the Laws of Ecclesiastical Polity*, I.vii. pp. 3-6, ed. Christopher Morris, 2 vols. (London, 1965), I, pp. 170-3; Calvin, *Institutes*, II.ii, pp. 2-4, 26-7.

34. Perry Miller, *The New England Mind: The Seventeenth Century* (Cambridge, Mass., 1954), p. 181 and ch. 6 generally; Calvin, *Institutes*, IV.vi, pp. 3,5; II.v, p. 1.

35. *A Grain of Mustard Seed* (1597), *The Work of William Perkins*, ed. Ian Breward (Abingdon, 1970), p. 393.

36. Torquato Tasso, *Discourses on the Heroic Poem*, translated by Mariella Cavalchini and Irene Samuel (Oxford, 1973), pp. 43-4; *Seneca, his Tenne Tragedies*, ed. Thomas Newton, 2 vols. (New York, 1967), I, pp. 4-5.

37. Anthony Giddens, *Central Problems in Social Theory* (London, 1979), pp. 193-5.

38. 'A Treatie of Human Learning,' stanzas 111-15, in *Poems and Dramas of Fulke Greville*, ed. Geoffrey Bullough, 2 vols. (Edinburgh, 1939); *Life*, pp. 164-5, 3.

39. *The Complete Works of Percy Bysshe Shelley*, ed. Thomas Hutchinson (Oxford, 1943), p. 441; W.B. Yeats, *Collected Poems* (London, 1933), p. 150; Sir Arthur Quiller-Couch, *On the Art of Writing* (Cambridge, 1946), pp. 34-5.

40. John Fekete, *The Critical Twilight* (London, 1977), p. 195. See also my article, 'Against Appropriation,' *Essays in Criticism*, XXXI (1981), pp. 181-95.

41. John Buxton, *Sir Philip Sidney and the English Renaissance* (London and New York, 1965), pp. 54-5.

42. *Report of the Central Committee of the CPSU to the XXVI Congress of the Communist Party of the Soviet Union*, delivered by L.I. Brezhnev (Moscow, 1981), pp. 110-11.

INDEX

Alberti, Leon Battista 11-12
Althusser, Louis 70, 74, 125
Apologie for Poetrie (Sidney) see *Defence of Poesie*
Arcadia, The (Sidney) 10, 15 26, 34-43, 78, 114, 133, 137-8
Aristotle and Aristotelianism 3-4, 6-14, 39-41, 47, 103, 126
Astrophil and Stella (Sidney) 15, 17-18, 21-24, 29-31, 35, 37, 44-55, 56-66, 69-83, 85-94, 95-109, 113-122, 137-38
Augustine, Saint 49, 60, 92

Bakhtin, Mikhail 70-1, 133
Barthes, Roland 75
Becon, Thomas 127-8, 135
Bloom, Harold 111, 113
Boethius 19, 25
Booth, Wayne 59
Brezhnev, Leonid 140
Burckhardt, Jacob 70, 80-1
Burke, Kenneth 44, 91
Buxton, John 139

Calvin, John 126-7, 130, 135-6, 139
Catullus 57-8, 60, 63
Certain Sonnets (Sidney) 18, 24, 26-29, 31
Cicero 12-14, 33
Cotter, James 30, 109 (n. 14)
Craig, D.H. 124

Dante Alighieri 6, 19, 20, 25
Defence of Poesie (Sidney) 1-17, 29, 34-37, 39-40, 50, 59-60, 98-104, 108 (n. 7, 10, 12), 124-43
DeNeef, A. Leigh 99
Descartes, René 73, 76
Donne, John 48, 62, 78, 109 (n. 16), 112, 119-21
Dryden, John 8, 16 (n. 3)
du Bartas, Guillaume 128, 139, 141 (n. 16)
du Plessis-Mornay, Philippe 131, 139
Durling, Robert 87

Eagleton, Terry 130
Elizabeth I, Queen 61, 125-6, 132
Ellmann, Richard 84
Erasmus, Desiderius 14

Fekete, John 139
Ferguson, Margaret 98-9, 108 (n. 7, 10)
Foucault, Michel 70, 72, 74, 77, 82
Fowler, Alastair 30, 92
Freccero, John 75, 92-3

Gascoigne, George 23-4, 29
Gentili, Vanna 29, 62-3 65 (n. 6)
Giddens, Anthony 137
Golding, Arthur 138
Googe, Barnabe 17, 21-24, 30

145

Index

Gosson, Stephen 134
Gramsci, Antonio 130
Greenblatt, Stephen 77
Greene, Robert 66 (n. 33), 112
Greville, Fulke 15, 24, 46, 69, 78, 113-15, 118, 132, 138-39

Hall, Stuart 125, 130
Hamilton, A.C. 102, 107 (n. 3), 109 (n. 16)
Hardison, O.B. 108 (n. 12), 124
Harington, John 129
Herbert, George 26, 69, 79, 121-2
Hercules 100-1, 108 (n. 12), 134
Homer 12, 42, 59, 134
Horace 9, 11, 35, 39-40
Humphrey, Lawrence 131, 134-5

Jameson, Frederic 80
Jones, Ann, and Peter Stallybrass 79
Jonson, Ben 30, 39, 112, 119, 121

Kalstone, David 30, 58
Krieger, Murray 61-2, 95-6, 102, 107 (n. 2, 3)
Kristeva, Julia 70-1

Lacan, Jacques 71-2, 74
Lady of May (Sidney) 126, 132
Landino, Cristoforo 5, 6, 16 (n. 2)
Lanham, Richard 44, 91
Languet, Hubert 59, 131-2
Levao, Ronald 99
Lewalski, Barbara 78
Lewis, C.S. 92
Luther, Martin 126

Macherey, Pierre 70, 76, 80-1
Machiavelli, Niccolo 134
Marlowe, Christopher 112
Marotti, Arthur 70
Martz, Louis L. 66 (n. 24)
Marvell, Andrew 47
Marx, Karl 71
McCoy, Richard C. 57, 70, 76

Miller, Jacqueline T. 54 (n. 4), 70
Mills, C. Wright 124-5
Milton, John 38, 133
Montaigne, Michel de 78
Montgomery, Robert L. 60

Nashe, Thomas 41, 92, 112
Nathan, Leonard 21
Nietzsche, Freidrich 74
Newton, Thomas 137
Nichols, J.G. 63

Ovid 18-19, 25, 58, 88, 127, 129

Perkins, William 133-34, 136
Petrarch and Petrarchanism 18-27, 29-32, 45-48, 51, 54 (n. 1), 59-63, 69-83, 84-94, 107 (n. 3), 110, 112, 118, 127
Philostratus 12
Plato and Platonism 3-9, 12, 15, 39-40, 45, 58, 88, 126, 128-29
Plutarch 9-12
Propertius 19, 56-7, 60
Protestantism 3, 6-7, 15, 66 (n. 23), 69-71, 76-80, 104, 112, 124-39
Puttenham, George 36, 100, 128-9
Putzel, Max 57, 63

Quiller-Couch, Arthur 138-9
Quintilian 13-14

Raitiere, Martin N. 124
Rebholz, Ronald 112
Rich, Penelope 44-5, 47, 73, 98
Roche, Thomas P., Jr. 30, 56-8
Ronsard, Pierre de 32, 53
Rudenstine, Neil 54 (n. 5), 62, 98, 107 (n. 3)

Shakespeare, William 24, 58, 63, 112, 115-19
Shepherd, Geoffrey 101, 109 (n. 14)
Sinfield, Alan 55 (n. 7), 58, 61, 64, 76, 80-1
Smith, Hallett 51, 55 (n. 6),

98
Spenser, Edmund 6, 10, 18, 24, 29, 38, 53, 61, 69, 78-79, 112, 133
Stone, Lawrence 126
Tasso 137
Tottel's Miscellany 18, 20, 26, 71
Troilus and Criseyde (Chaucer) 24
Turbervile, George 17-18, 21-25, 30
Vance, Eugene 75
Waller, Gary 91, 97-8, 102, 107 (n. 4), 108 (n. 7), 113, 124
Walzer, Michael 130-32
Warkentin, Germaine 62, 75
Waswo, Richard 115
Weiner, Andrew 54 (n. 3), 66 (n. 23), 76, 141 (n. 14)
Williams, Raymond 80
Wilson, Thomas 13, 100, 127
Winters, Yvor 17-18, 29
Wyatt, Thomas 29, 75, 77-8
Young, Richard B. 54 (n. 4), 63, 102, 104, 109 (n. 18)
Zumthor, Paul 25, 76

For Product Safety Concerns and Information please contact our EU representative GPSR@taylorandfrancis.com
Taylor & Francis Verlag GmbH, Kaufingerstraße 24, 80331 München, Germany

www.ingramcontent.com/pod-product-compliance
Lightning Source LLC
Chambersburg PA
CBHW061452300426
44114CB00014B/1940